A

Boomer

Bible

(All 5 books)

K. A. Champagne

Version

Not Divinely Inspired

Other books by K.A. Champagne:

Ages 2-5 for babysitters or adults to read to the little ones:

WE NEED A NAP! Series, 2019
Maurice the Cat
Manny the Moth
Dumblebee the Bumblebee
Larry the Lizard
Steve the Scatterbrained Squirrel
Dawn the Sleeping Fawn
Joe the Crow

Thank you Note to a Squirrel, 2020

DOES ANYBODY KNOW? Series, 2021
Where Roaches Go?
Why'd They Name a Woodpecker Whisper?

Dog Lovers ages 12+:

Spirit Lost, Spirit Found, My Story by Me, Spirit The Dog! 2020
(we helped with the typing)

Young adolescents ages 7-12:

The Thought Green Room, 2019
The Keeper of the Truth in The Land of Words, 2020

Adults only ages 18+. Contains adult language or subject matter:

Thoughts from Inside the Shell, 2020
Crack the Shell Wide Open, 2020
Shell Fragments, 2020
Shell Dust, 2021
Farewell to the Shell, 2021
Middle Child, 2022

All books available on Amazon.com

Dedication

As with all of my books, I'd like to
dedicate my work to the people who,
don't get me,
don't like me,
don't need me,
don't care if they hurt me,
can't forgive me
And didn't hire me.
Thank you for your inspiration.

Table of Contents

Preface

Most of my life was spent over my head and out of my league. I don't remember having a comfort zone. I placed my ignorant, uneducated or barely educated ass in the middle of some of the wealthiest, best educated people on Earth. Men and women who felt comfortable in any situation. I found myself embarrassing my way to the top. Learning as I went along. No one held my hand. I suffered alone and I learned.

All of the wisdom in "A Boomer Bible" was earned. And believe me, some of it was costly and none of it came easy.

ACKNOWLEDGEMENTS

Special thanks to the "Digital Navigators" at the Arizona Library Tech Access Phone Line and KDP Customer Service.

Introduction

A Boomer Bible

"A Boomer Bible" contains all 5 of the manuscripts that came to be known as "The Shell Books." "The Shell Books," were pieces of journals I kept over a 50 year period. Like the Bible, "The Shell Books" will not only tell you how to live life but they will also tell you how NOT to live life. Just like the Bible there will be poetry and bizarre stories. They touch on pretty much every subject a baby boomer had to deal with from the beginning to the end. And like the Bible, there's even a letter to the Corinthians.

Some of the stories in "The Shell Books" come with pictures. No pictures in the Bible. While there is something in each of "The Shell Books" to enlighten you, I never claim that "The Shell Books" are "divinely inspired." You may say to yourself, how important can these books be? I've never heard of this guy. Let me put it this way, DON'T read the books and see how it goes. Then read them and see how it goes. I think you'll see the difference they make in your day to day. And no, you won't burn in Hell if you don't read them but maybe if you are of a certain age, they'll show you a little glimpse of YOUR past.

Like the writers of the Bible, I give my opinions using the best information available at the time. And yes, just like in the Bible there's even a miracle, ME.

Most of the pieces in "The Shell Books" were written right after they occurred, with no time for the stories or feelings to change. The stories in the Bible were passed down by oral history and weren't actually written down until 30-40 years later and not by the people who actually witnessed the events. See any problems with that?

Now I realize that most of you learned about the Bible from your mothers. Well, I'm not putting your mothers down, I'm sure they did the best they could with the information available at the time. Society has learned so much more about the origins of the Universe since your mothers were in school. So I'm not putting down your momma or my own, I'm just updating the information. Just like the Bible, you can take it or leave it. I see the stories in "A Boomer Bible" as honest examples of what to do and what not to do, what to say and what not to say, how to act and how not to act. And I'll make you one promise,

7

"A Boomer Bible" will be a lot more fun to read than the actual Bible.

If I were famous, "A Boomer Bible" would be revered by many as a wonderfully in depth look into the thoughts of an important figure. Since I'm not famous, you'll have to trust me. And remember, Jesus wasn't famous until he was.

They were written in this order:

Thoughts from Inside the Shell
Crack the Shell Wide Open
Shell Fragments
Shell Dust
Farewell to the Shell

Addendum: I put "A Boomer Bible" together for many reasons. One reason was to prove that any idiot can compile writings and call it a bible or in this case, "A Boomer Bible."
Be careful what you believe, it might just be made up.

This is the book I lived by

This book, "A Boomer Bible," should be read cover to cover or not at all. There's so much that lies between the lines. The introduction is as important as the acknowledgements. And in some cases, the acknowledgments are as important as the text. So don't cheat yourself.

Now, Roberta tells me that I shouldn't tell people how to read my books. Obviously, I feel differently. I would've loved to have had instructions before reading a book. But look, I don't think you'll die if you don't read any of my books from cover to cover.

However, I should tell you about "The Curse." No, maybe not. Wait, I'll tell you this much. There is a curse, it has been in effect for many years but it only applies to those who are actually mean to me. I think you're safe if you don't read the book the way I suggest. I would, however, think twice before sending me a negative comment. You need to know that I don't control "The Curse." But it's real. So be nice.

Thank you.

Book I

Thoughts from Inside the Shell

PG

If our parents don't guide us,
WE have to create
meaning in our lives.
That is our first job.

KC

✤ ✤ ✤ ✤ ✤ ✤ ✤

The Age of Awareness

The greatest sadness in my life is racism
and bigotry. My personal failures and
disappointments seem to fade with time
but I've seen the ugly face of racism and
bigotry everyday since the
age of awareness.

KC

12:28 AM

Can't sleep.

It sucks being a sensitive person.
Most people don't understand
This affliction at all.

You are made fun of...
Grown tired of...
And always seem to be embarrassed...

Noises seem **louder**
Lights seem **brighter**
Cold seems **colder**
Hot seems **hotter**
Hunger seems **hungrier**
Feelings are **hurt easier**

And there doesn't seem to be a pill
you can take to correct it.

Kenny

There have been times in my life that I could
control or keep the attention of
a whole room full of people.
Only to be followed by the exact opposite.
Insecure, shy, sad, negative,
depressed, weak.
I don't know why any of these traits appear
in me from time to time.
They also choose when and for how long
each is in charge.

"The Shell Books"
are possibly different from
anything you've ever read.
They can be helpful to you on many levels.
If worse comes to worse, you can
think and say bad things about me
and feel superior.

Why we Love Stephanie

"With every passing day an old white man longing for an America of yesteryear dies. And a bunch of young, diverse people are turning eighteen and they are sick of school shootings; they want to have sex and not get pregnant and they damn well know there's not a transgender basketball team plotting to end the big game.

Stehanie Ruhle-MSNBC

Child Rearing

If you raise your children the way your mother raised you, they will end up 2 generations behind by the time they are 21.

End of Night

Was it the morning?
Or just the end of night?

What was I thinking?
Was it wrong or was it right?

How would I know?
Would someone come forward and say?

Was it the end of night?
Or just the start of day?

Three AM

Lonely	is late night phone calls
Lonely	is too much to drink
Lonely	is off the wall
Lonely	is me I think
Lonely	is bitter
Lonely	is scared
Lonely	is sitting alone in his chair
Lonely	is all the time
Lonely	is a friend of mine
Lonely	will sit with me and stare
Lonely	wears only his underwear
Lonely	has no respect
Lonely	is a nervous wreck
Lonely	may want to leave but
Lonely	will always be back

Gone Fishin'

I've had my fill of surgeons
found most as cold as sturgeons

They hit you with life changing drama
just the opposite of President Obama

seeming to care less about the trauma
to husband, wife and momma

We are faceless nameless body parts
pancreas, livers and broken hearts

No time for feelings
Less time to care

Insert the IV and
shave the hair

-

KC
11/18

Dead End

Just wait 'til you turn the corner my friend
the corner of life that leads to the end
on the street where everything that
worked is broken
where nature is real
and she ain't jokin'
where no one is spared
not even a token

when you realize
maybe halfway down
there's no way to stop it
there's no way to slow down

Let's see how you act
when you see it's a fact
that you're reaching the
end
and there's no turning back

KC
11/18

ALONE

Sexual Healing

When voting, I really don't care what's between a person's legs or who they share it with. I care that they can do the job of governing.

Guilty!

If I were a black person, I would've thrown an Elizabeth Holmes sentencing party. Finally a rich, attractive, white girl goes to jail for something she did wrong.

THE GIFT

MOST PEOPLE WILL HAVE LITTLE TIME

FOR THEMSELVES.

1–18

BELONGS TO SCHOOL AND PARENTS.

18–65

BELONGS TO WORK, FAMILY, KIDS, ETC.

65 TO 75

IF YOU GET TO THESE YEARS,

YOU'RE LUCKY.

SO YOU MAY GET 10 YEARS

OF A 75 YEAR LIFE FOR YOURSELF.

HEALTH ?

DO YOU STILL THINK LIFE IS A GIFT?

When push came to shove

She was a gay woman
who fell in love with a man
and nobody she knew
could help her understand
His name was Jack
and he loved her back
so what the hell's a girl supposed to do
She was a gay woman
what could she do
She really loved Jack
and he loved her too
But when push
came to shove
push got it's way
and shoved old Jack
right out of the way

Aging

Your titties are sagging
My ball sack too
And there's absolutely nothing
that we can do

We're aging

The process started many years ago
It will happen to every living soul you know

Aging

Long ago my skin looked fine
Now it doesn't even look like mine

Aging

My hair fell out long ago
Why it happened i think i know

Aging

But now there is an alternative to aging
they say
The scientists say they'll release it one day
But until they do
We'll all be
Aging

Double Deuces

Everybody's cute at 22
There really isn't much
that you have to do
Just show up
with a smile on your face
Make it look like you
belong in this place
Say something nice
they'll invite you back
These words are true
it's just a natural fact
Everybody's cute at 22

LIFE LESSONS

MANY YEARS AGO WHEN I ASKED MY
FRIEND, RACE TRACK RALPH,
IF HE HAD ANY ENEMIES,
HIS RESPONSE WAS:
"YOU DON'T GET TO BE FORTY
WITHOUT PISSING SOMEONE OFF."
RIP BROTHER

Open your Mind

I've watched what pure
unbridled capitalism can do.
I've also seen the damage pure
socialism can do.
But a hybrid of both might just be the
answer we're looking for.

There's nothing a white guy with a penny
hates more than a nigger with a nickel.

Chris Rock

Musicians

If I would've had children,
I would've steered them toward
being musicians.
Because you can only tell a joke once.

Old people cursing:

Damn it to Hell
Kiss my ass
Blow it out your ass
For Christ's sakes
Son of a bitch
You bastid

Young people cursing:

Fuck you
Eat me
Blow me
Bite me
Suck my ass
You cunt

Team Spirit

You might just be like the people you're
putting down. Maybe the color of the
jerseys are the only difference.

The Titanic

People are like icebergs.
You rarely see what dangers lay
beneath the surface.
Remember this and you'll save yourself
from a lot of grief.
Charm is usually nothing more
than a costume worn when convenient.

GUN VIOLENCE

Mourn the victim, that's all we do.
The real crime is, that's all we do.

Kindness can be profitable.
A lack of *kindness* can be costly.

It doesn't matter

It really doesn't

If someone is kind to me,
I don't care what they look like or
where they're from.
If someone is mean to me, I don't
care what they look like or where
they're from.

What's to come?

The future will overtake the past.
It always does. And you'll either be
a part of it
or you won't.

The key to a long marriage is forgiveness.
That's it.

Vicey Versey

What do you owe a person that you've
never met before?
The answer is, the same treatment that
you would appreciate.
Yes, it's that simple.
Plus, the best tasks are the ones
you do for free.

The Good Samaritan

The good samaritan story
proves that you don't need Jesus
to do good works.
The good samaritan had never
heard of Jesus.

For J.O.S.H.

I'd like to let you love me
if that is what you wish
if it's love that you desire
then I can grant your wish

but understand the meaning
of what you really love
is it me that you desire
or this dream from up above

for I am not a love song
or a movie with sunsets bright
I'm just this contradiction
this good versus evil fight

if this last remark confuses you
I'll try my best to explain
I'm just this little boy
who's trying to be a man

I'm an addict who refrains from drugs
an alcoholic that doesn't drink
a comic with a tear in his eye
a pen run out of ink

a counselor in need of much advice
a gentleman who is rude
a commitment not kept from time to time
a mistake that's tried and true

but if it's me you think you love
make sure you understand
that I'm no savior from up above
I'm just an ordinary man

BLACK FRIDAY

Spend it on this
Spend it on that
Spend it on food
and you'll only get fat

Spend it on others
Spend on the days
Father's and Mother's
whatever the craze

Spend it on me
Spend it on you

Conditioned to Spend
that's what we are
think you have it all
and they keep raising the bar

More   More   More
that's what you need
this is a monster
you continue to feed

and when it's all spent what then will you do?
if you let marketing become your new guru?

I've Been

I've been a wonderful man
I've been a despicable man
A rare in the middle man
extremely this
extremely that
extremely skinny
extremely fat
I've been a crazy man
extremely lazy man
a get it done man
a no quit man and
I've had enough of all this shit man
I've been a quiet man
I've been a lonely man
and not just an alone man
I hope you understand
but I'm not sure that you can
unless you can see the other man

Like Father, Like Son

Robbie Knievel just died
His father was a daredevil
His father was Evel
Robbie became a daredevil
George W Bush was a politician
His father, George HW Bush
was a politician
My father was a verbally abusive drunk
So I became a verbally abusive drunk
Your children will be what you are
Chris Wallace is a questioner of people
Mike, his dad, was a questioner of people
And so it goes

2023

You're 30 years younger than me.
You have a title and a college degree.
You make a decent amount of money.
You have all the conveniences of
"the good life."
I would still rather be me,
over 70, than to have to face
the next 30 years on Earth.

Music

The only thing the boomers got right.
The reason is, we did drugs.
Marijuana makes you more creative.
Alcohol makes you stupid.

Successful Writer

I've written and published pretty much
everything that I've wanted to write.
That's success.

The 10 stupidest human activities:

Rock climbing

Religion

Rodeos

Gambling

Funerals

Shark week

Hairdos

Banning dogs from anywhere

Keeping sexuality a secret

Driving when you could walk

Here's what I've learned over seventy years,
you may not want to hear it but it's true.
If you don't make them cum or laugh,
most women see no use for men anymore.
In the old days I would've added
money to the list. But not anymore.

ChatGPT

Over the years, I've sent my
books to some of the best
writers in America.
Some of them were very famous.
This is a message to those of
you who were dismissive
of my books.
Looks like we've become equals.
ChatGPT has leveled
the writing field.
The World doesn't need
writers anymore.
Karma is making all of us
irrelevant.

Thank you for your kindness,
you pretentious bastards.

I take little solace from the
fact that "ChatGPT" makes
all writers seem unnecessary.
Just like some people feel about
"The Shell Books."

Anniversaries

Columbine 1999

Virginia Tech 2007

Aurora CO 2012

Mother Emanuel AME Church 2015

Sandy Hook 2012

Las Vegas 2017

Pulse Nightclub 2016

Gabby Giffords, Safeway, Tucson 2011

First Baptist Church TX 2017

Uvalde TX 2022

Michigan State 2023

Monterey Park CA 2023

Parkland 2018

El Paso Walmart 2019

And the hits just keep on coming

Keep voting REPUBLICAN

And we all might die in a mass shooting.

The Real Problem

You do realize that it doesn't really
matter if they're crazy as long as
they can't buy a gun.
There are crazy people all over the World.
But they can't shoot up the grocery store
if they can't buy a gun.

School Days

Civilization as I knew it
has changed. Everyone seems to
have a gun,no matter their
age or background.
A 6 year old just shot
his first grade teacher.
This is what "civilization" has
come to in 2023.

Catch 22

I caught 22 but then I missed 23.
Never even saw 21.

Two

There are only two
human characteristics that
never grow old.
One is behavioral.
It is your INTEGRITY.
One is physical. It is your SMILE.
They are of EQUAL importance.

HAHAHAHAHA!

I stopped caring about what my peers
thought of me many years ago.
Can you imagine just how worthless
their opinions are to me now?

My opinions matter.
Maybe not to you but they matter
to the people who matter.

Kindness Pays

People will work for little or nothing if
they enjoy the work. Some will even work
for free if you treat them with respect.

They put the kibosh on it

I realized over my lifetime
that I could override a kibosh.
It's not easy but it can be done.

The Pale

What's before the pale?
I've been beyond.

Mean Girls

You lied to him
You probably laughed at him
You talked about him
when he wasn't present
And you never
showed him any respect
That makes you the asshole

I think I just saw Elizabeth Hurley's
bikini shot from the nursing home.
She really lights up a walker.

Uncouth

There was no couth in the
neighborhood I was raised in.
How was I supposed to learn couth?

Every Evening
LIST THE GUN DEATHS DAILY
I believe that there should be
a daily gun death count broadcast
by every network. EVERY DAY.
CNN, MSNBC, and even FOX news
along with local broadcasts.
This was done years ago
during the VietNam war.
We are killing about **a thousand a week.**
I think we should show it.

Superbowl Party
If it's white kids, it's called a celebration.

If it's black kids, it's a riot.

Where's the Horse Shit?
Why is it that you never see horse shit
in old westerns? What's up with that?
The horses never shit.

42

I'm Crazy

I'm crazy and I know it
Others know it too
Some of my crazy is fun
Some of my crazy is ugly
I'm crazy
I fit in with crazy people
I like it sometimes
Sometimes I don't
I can't always control it
Because I'm crazy

I'm not at all afraid of being dead.
It's the moments right before death
that frighten me.

Don't blame me

When I was coming up, misogyny was
like cigarettes, accepted
and promoted. It took years for me
to understand both addictions.

THERE GOES THE NEIGHBORHOOD

Too many MAGA

In this neighborhood

Too many MAGA

And man, that's not good

No sense

of right and wrong

No taste at all

Too many MAGA

this place is bound to fall

d rump
All my life I thought it was me.
Then d rump became President
and explained everything.

I don't like funerals.
I guess I'm just not a mourning person.

Heartache Is
Heartache is raceless, colorless,
genderless, religionless, sexless.
Heartache is worldwide.

The world has already changed forever.
The notice just hasn't gone out yet.

You can't spell religion without the EGO

"If you gave (Jerry) Falwell an enema,
he could be buried in a matchbox."

Christopher Hitchens on Fallwell

The Dark Ages

Allowing religious zealots to run the
World has been tried before.
It's known as "The Dark Ages"
for a reason.

When Religion becomes Political,
it ceases to be a spiritual experience
and becomes politics.

Was Jesus more of a
Socialist or a Capitalist?
Christians can't have it both ways.
Either follow His teachings,
or quit identifying as a Christian.

Jesus H. Christ!

Jesus and I would've been cool. I agree with most everything he stood for and I especially liked the magic. But like a lot of people who start to get a following, history tells us that he started thinking he was God. Allegedly, he even started claiming to be the son of God in public. That's when I would have chimed in, " Hey man, I think you need to slow down." But as we know he didn't.

Now the people who call themselves Christians today, show very little if any resemblance to the teachings that Jesus preached many years ago. Like I've stated many times before, while I believe a dude named Jesus existed years ago, I do not believe a God of any sort has ever walked on Earth.

Paraphrasing Christopher Hitchens:
Religions make people OK
with being subservient.

Christopher Hitchens

I learned a lot of truth from
Christopher Hitchens.
He might've been the most educated and
knowledgeable person of his generation.
Although his formal education came from
Oxford, a lot of his knowledge
came from living it,
from personally being there.
He was brilliant, entertaining and
wonderfully rude at times.
I highly recommend spending some time with
Christopher Hitchens on YouTube.
He validated beliefs that I've held
for many years.
Only the good die young.
RIP Mr Hitchens
and thank you for sharing your courage.

GOD?

"When God is used to explain everything,
it explains nothing."
Christopher Hitchens

Paraphrasing Christopher Hitchens again:
Fascism is another word for the
Christian right wing of the Catholic Church.

4200

That's how many religions
there are in the World.
And they all believe that theirs
will give them eternal life.
If religion isn't man made,
why are there so many versions?
I lost all respect for religion,
all 4200 of them, after I discovered
what they're really all about
and it ain't salvation.

ST ANTHONY

DO YOU REALLY BELIEVE THAT THERE IS A GUY
NAMED ANTHONY UP IN THE CLOUDS
WAITING FOR YOU TO LOSE SOMETHING
SO HE CAN SPRING INTO ACTION
AND HELP YOU FIND IT?
MY MOTHER DID.

The Unchurch

I quit praying over 30 years ago.
During that time,
more than a few things happened:
Hurricane Katrina destroyed
New Orleans,
I had some serious health problems,
I got married,
my wife and I found Spirit the dog
and together we had more money
than we needed.
And neither one of us,
both alcoholics,
has had to drink again.
Didn't ask a God for any of it.
Now when someone gets shot,
you offer thoughts and prayers.
But people keep getting shot.
Maybe YOU should stop praying
and start **voting.**

Do you really know or are you just hoping?

No man, not me

Even though I don't believe any of the
"God" stories, it doesn't mean I don't
believe in being humble.
You see, I don't believe you have to
make up fantastical stories to be
a good neighbor.
You can believe those
far fetched stories
and look down on people who don't.
But I'll promise you one thing,
when you die,
that's all she wrote.

While I've come to believe that
religious people are either naive or
lazy, I'll always agree to something
that makes you a kind person.

Indoctrination

There will probably come a time during your
life when events will shake you to your core. Just
being told this truth can be of help to you during
these times. I personally have been shaken to
that degree on more
than one occasion.
It can knock you senseless.
You may have to sit down.
GOD'S will!
When I was young and naive, I was told,
look around, you can see GOD in everything.
I believed that fairy tale. As I got older and
actually saw the truth, I no longer saw
GOD but rather FACT.
I have since adjusted my belief system.
I am finally okay with the END being
the END.

Dear White Supremacists,
   What is the color of an immortal soul?

Letter to the Corinthians

Dear Corinthians,

Cut the crap!

Paul

Faith

I just find it hard to believe
that there's an invisible dictator
up in the clouds watching every move
I make in order to pass judgment
on me after I die.
If you want to base your life
on a book written by who knows who,
Well, that's your business.
Just don't try to force
your insanity on me.

And now, some One Liners....

I either made them all up or heard them from someone else but don't remember who. If it's the latter, sorry. Either way, some of them are pretty great!
Hope you enjoy my version of what I call,

"Edgy Mark Twain"

Life IS Fair—
sooner or later it breaks everyone's heart.

You will need help from a stranger one day.

Why do Nazi sympathizers love the Republican Party so much?

Everyone is an equal when the doctor says,
"Sorry, but you've got stage 4 Cancer."

Once you know,
you can't unknow.

Captain Apathy
has all the powers of Superman
but absolutely no desire to use them.

Most everyone that you pay attention to
will change your life,
even if it's just a little.

"Time" Traders

We all trade our "time" for money
but it's the time
that holds the real value.

If you keep voting Republican,
the young girls in your life will have
no rights by the time they're 21.

I figure that if I'm not dead,
I don't have any extra money.

I have sadly come to the conclusion
that if you live long enough,
everyone you know
will eventually let you down.

Until it is, it isn't.

While honesty may hurt my feelings,
dishonesty will piss me off
and hurt my feelings.

New friends let you be
what your old friends won't.

I'm very famous
to some very unfamous people.

Ego is the most costly human trait.

Since you're the one who made the list long,
you're the one who can shorten it.

Republican women are like cockroaches
voting FOR pesticide.
Sunny Hostin, The View

I've never been offended by kindness.

If one sentence in a book changes your life,
the cost of the book becomes irrelevant.

Big **DICK**
or
Big **GUN,**
you don't need **both.**

Time is the only thing you're really
running out of.

MONEY IS THE THIEF THAT WILL STEAL
YOUR LIFE IF YOU LET IT.

IN MY TWENTIES SEX WAS EVERYTHING BUT
FOOD.

I'm starting to think that shock isn't even
a human experience anymore.

You can waste time hating who you disagree
with or you can learn something new.

If I have one suggestion,
it would be to make some NEW friends.

If you were really the "smarter" sibling,
you would be building the others up.

I've been called an asshole so many times
that I started thinking of it as an
attractive body part.

The Bible continues to get people killed.

If you were raised in the suburbs, got
married and moved to another suburb,
don't even talk to me about "life."

Many women make themselves
sex objects
with all the powder and paint.

One of the things that I'm most proud of
is that I didn't buy everything
that the marketing wanted me to.

The Bible is a relic
that humanity must move past
in order to grow.

I've never heard a woman say,
"You only want me for my brains."

Does anyone know exactly when
the cows come home?

Sometimes you'll have to
remind your wife that,
"this is the best
that both of us could do."

KC

Imagine living during the time in history
when the US mail
was the fastest way to communicate.

Always remember,
eventually no one's opinion matters.

It takes less time to say thank you
than it does to wait at a traffic light.

What if rejection was a good feeling?

What if the gas inside of farts was colored?

Conservatives keep society from
reaching its full potential.

I talk about being a very sensitive person
but be careful, I've been training myself to
be cold and bold.

Iconic is iconic.

Heroin and Technology,
they both make the user feel great at first.

One side of Alcoholism was a blast.

There were no "altar girls"
when I was young.

Titles
What they give employees instead of money.

Republicans
Christians who would really rather not
help others.

Please treat these books the way you would want
your books to be treated.

Ya know, if Roberta and I had friends,
I bet they'd be impressed with us.

Basic directions for anything in 2022:
Did you try unplugging it?

Just Do It

The way to become an author is to write
something and publish it. The way to
become a poet is to write poetry
and publish it.

I've said it once and I'll say it again, in the
future "The Shell Books" should be
handled with white gloves only. No latex.

II

Crack the Shell
W i d e O p e n

AMERICAN FAMILY VALUES
(not necessarily in this order)

The ones we call "Legacy Americans"
These are the direct descendants of the people
who came here and killed the natives,
then stole their land.

The ones we call the "Racists"
These are the descendants of the people who
brought the slaves from Africa.
They beat and tortured them in order to build
our great country for free.

The ones we call the "Religious"
These are the naive ones,
the ones that need to be told what to do.
These people think that there is
an "Invisible Dictator" up in the clouds.

The ones we call the "2nd Amendmenters"
These are the ones that value guns
over human life.

The ones we call the "Right to Lifers"
These are the people who believe women
should be forced to give birth.
I call them "Forced Birthers."
Wait til they reap what they sow.

The Life Part

Where and how it starts has a lot to do with
the degree of difficulty.

—

KC

A lot of people suffer.
A few have a good time.
They all

Die

If the above statement bothers you,
DO NOT READ ANY FURTHER!
I promised this book would be honest.

UNFAMOUS

I AM FAMOUSLY *UNFAMOUS*
THAT'S THE WAY I'D LIKE TO STAY
FROM WHAT I'VE SEEN OF LIFE
TO *FAME* I SAY, *"NO WAY"*

I CAN SAY WHAT I WANT TO
GO ANYWHERE I PLEASE
AND BECAUSE NO ONE KNOWS ME
I GET AROUND WITH EASE

I LIKE TO BE *UNKNOWN* I SAY
IT'S FUN TO BE *UNKNOWN* TODAY
I HOPE THAT NO ONE EVER KNOWS
WHO WROTE THESE

"SOON TO BE UNFAMOUS"
POEMS AND PROSE

Pablo & Vincent

Every time someone says to me
that my writing is stupid,
that some of my thoughts are offensive
or they just don't get it,
I remember I once heard that Picasso was
told that if he could "just straighten it out,"
the painting would be great.

*I'm also reminded of the fact that Vincent
never sold a painting while he was alive.*

Along those same lines,
recently I discovered that Sidney Greenstreet,
the famous actor from the Maltese Falcon
and other iconic films,
didn't make his first film until age 61.

Feelings

I discovered many years ago that
one of my roles in life is to make

people feel.

I was at a Mardi Gras Ball and my
best friend's older brother said
to me out of the blue:
"Ya' know Kenny, you make

people feel.

You don't always make 'em

feel good

but you make 'em

feel."

Although it probably wasn't meant
as a compliment,
I decided to make it one anyway.

Why I publish

Although the thought of rejection passed through my mind, I realized that I could no longer *be afraid.*
Meaningful art takes chances.

—

KC

Throughout the "Shell Books" books, I've quoted people who I'm fond of, whose work I've looked up to for a long time, whose public persona is what I wish I could be.

K̄C

"Putting something creative in the world risks not everyone applauding. There is no courage in criticizing the creative. There is only courage in creating the creative and trusting that vulnerability over to others."

—

Dan LeBatard

74

Birth

I know you didn't ask to be here
You know, neither did I
And on more than one occasion
I found myself asking why

But for some unknown reason
I didn't quit
eating my daily dose of life's bullshit
I got up everyday (pretty much)
and paid the price you pay

And although
I didn't always do what I was told
for some unknown reason
I've managed to get old

Follow what they tell you
do exactly what they say
but be prepared for trouble
if you question things along the way

And Everything In Between

I've had a gun against my head in the housing projects of New Orleans. I've stood on the roof of the Pentagon and in the Office of the Joint Chiefs. I've been drunk in the gutter on Bourbon St and I've been given a guided tour of the White House. Can you imagine what happened in between?

My favorite Mark Twain quote:
"Travel is fatal to prejudice, bigotry and narrow mindedness."

Even with cable tv and the internet, most people don't think past their neighborhoods.

—
KC

Judgment Day

The only real fairness in life is
death!
I did not choose
the sperm and the egg that made me.
The DNA comes from others
not of my choosing.

Nor did I choose
the environment in which I was raised.
Or the events that formed me.

I did not choose
my teachers.

It's not fair to judge me harshly.

Judge my teachers.
They were forced upon me.

VERBAL VIOLENCE

I was raised in a
Verbally Violent House.
Afraid since the day I was seven.
Scared to even open my mouth.
Wasn't sure I'd be sent to Heaven.

Yes, I've committed *Verbal* Violence.
Just like my daddy did to me.
What I despised in my daddy,
seems like he passed it down to me.

I play the horses as bad as he did,
as if anyone plays them good.
If you asked if we should have a drink,
you know, I always said we should.

But he did one thing,
thank God I didn't do.
He had three children,
when he shouldn't have had two.

I was raised in a
Verbally Violent House.
Afraid since the day I was seven.
Scared to even open my mouth.
Wasn't sure I'd be sent to Heaven.

We are all what was done to us as children.

Although I obviously do not condone crime and violence, I do not believe human beings are born violent criminals. Nor do I believe that any race has a monopoly on evil.

Plus, we all want shit. If your parents can't or don't get you shit, eventually you will get your own shit,
anyway you can.
'Cause we all want shit.

Note: while I've seen some overcome their childhoods, many do not. Plus, we are all raised by our generations.

My Father
My Brothers
and Me

I come from a family of **Narcissists.**
self-love, the feeling we can't resist.
We demand it from you.
If you don't worship,
you're through.

I come from a family of **Narcissists.**
My father, my brothers, me, too.
I'm the first to admit it.
I keep hoping we quit it
but it's so hard to do.

we're so much better than you.

I'm extremely surprised to admit it.

Narcissism

Narcissists do not create themselves. I come from a family of passive/aggressive narcissists. It's passed down from one generation to the next. It's real and it's natural. It continues until one of the generations calls it out.
Narcissists are created in one of two ways:
1. During childhood you start to make yourself important if no one else does.
2. You are continually told how great you are. In other words, excessive adoration or excessive criticism.
Although **Narcissism** does not invoke sympathy, it is painful to the **Narcissist.** They can rarely admit that they are **Narcissistic.**
Without treatment or therapy, it will last a lifetime alienating almost everyone. While disdain is the easiest response, understanding can be more productive.

"We live in a racist country"

NBA Coach Greg Popovich

❧ ❧ ❧ ❧ ❧ ❧ ❧ ❧

"White men don't feel the effects of the 'ism's.'"

Megan Rapinoe World Cup Champion

❧ ❧ ❧ ❧ ❧ ❧ ❧ ❧

So many times I've heard,
"The 'good Muslims' should be speaking
out against ISIS."
But I rarely hear that,
"The 'good cops' should be speaking
out against the 'bad cops'. "
And one more,
what about the "good Christians"?
What should they do?

KC

Racism

Although I grew up surrounded by racism, I
almost immediately felt uncomfortable with it.
Even at a young age,
I saw no reason to
hate people I didn't know.

I've always felt that racism was pretty stupid.
I've lived in this country
long enough to know that
uneducated white people
are no different than
uneducated black people.

No race is superior to others.

While there are individuals in each race
who think they are superior,
like the Royal Family,

I'm pretty sure they also look
at the toilet paper
after they wipe their butts.

ELIJAH the violin player

He was just twenty-three
but he was dark don't you see.
Being black is a crime in this country.
While my white skin protects me
and no one rejects me,
he looked like HE did, not me.
You have to admit, you can't make up this shit.
I keep wishing it would stop but it don't.
And white folks can help but they won't.
Now we're all afraid
of this bed that we've made
and the fact it's been jammed down our throat.
He was just twenty-three.
Just as easily could've been me.
But my white skin protects me.
I walk down streets all the time.
But because I'm white it's not a crime.
My white skin protects me,
unlike Elijah at twenty-three.
Elijah McClain,
remember his name.
He could've been you or me.
I, too was quite strange
and quirky you see,
when I was a young man
of twenty-three.

There are people in America
raising their children to be
RACISTS.

K̄C

The part of life that I loved when I was
young is gone forever but sadly the part I
hated when I was young
is still going strong.

K̄C

If you force people to think more than
they're used to thinking,
it may just piss them off.

K̄C

WHITE PRIVILEGE

I started out with nothing but

WHITE SKIN

and that was enough to get my foot in the door.

Then I learned charm. Although I most definitely wasn't always charming, I now had an additional tool for success but it was that

WHITE SKIN

that made it all possible.

There were no blacks or women out of 36 sales reps at one of my sales jobs.

In addition to the 35

WHITE MEN

There was one Cuban- who worked Miami.

Chronic Pain

The only good thing
about pain,
Chronic Pain,
is that it liberates your
opinions.
It's kinda like having
"Fuck You Money"
without the cash.

Act Like You've Been There

Even though I've been there,
I've never been able
to act like I have.

Hometown

I was *from there*
but I wasn't really *of there.*
And some of you know what I mean.

I was *from there*
but I wasn't really *of there.*
Maybe that's why they all seemed so
mean.

For a while I thought I was a Kennedy,
sure they mixed up the babies.

'cause I was *from there*
but I really wasn't *of there.*
Maybe that's why they all seemed so
mean.
A few of you know what I mean.

A few of you know exactly what I mean.

Epilogue to Hometown

I wish I was proud of where I'm from
but I'm not.
I wish I had memories that differed
from the ones I got
but I don't.
I wish my mind would let me forget
but it won't.

The Other

When I was young I was taught
to fear the other
if not hate the other.
In my town, the other was **black.**
You know who the other is in your town.

We were taught that white
people
were superior to **black** people.
They were lesser beings.

Then I went out into the world and discovered
the other was just like me.

Happy Other's Day!

Prologue to John Wayne Man

One of my biggest questions about life
has always been,
who decided how things would be?
What gave them the right to make rules
for all human beings?
Men will act this way.
Women will act that way.
A person should act like their chronological age.
Men don't cry, why?

Who decided and why did we let them tell us
what to do or how to be?

The lives we live are ours.
The time is limited and you won't be refunded
at the end for time wasted.
Even if you are offended by a man who cries
on occasion, ask yourself this question:

Do I do anything that's offensive to others?

It's mostly all DNA and circumstance anyway.

When you think about it, all of us has something
that irritates someone else.

John Wayne Man

don't want to be no John Wayne Man
as you'll see I've taken a stand
not gonna be no John Wayne Man

wouldn't have made it in the old west
wasn't born to have a big hairy chest
just can't be no John Wayne Man

I've had all I can stand of that John Wayne Man
the one my father wanted me to be
it took many years to get over the fear
and to finally be set free

oh daddy, please don't make me fight
can't be no John Wayne Man *tonight*
I hoped one day you'd understand
I can't be no John Wayne Man

don't think I'm better
than the Asian or the black man
you see, I don't want to be no John Wayne Man

I've had all I can stand of that John Wayne Man
no bar room brawls for me
it took me some time
but my life is mine
the way it was meant to be

so when you see me cryin'
war medals won't be shinin'
you'll see that I'm not buying
that John Wayne Man

now if the issue really matters
and your life seems torn and tattered
I'll help you take a stand
but I can never be that John Wayne Man

Epilogue to John Wayne Man

Although it's true that I've never been very
good at any
form of confrontation,
(see pussy, wimp, punk, sissy....).
I still believe it takes more strength to walk
away from a fight,
in addition to the fact that it's healthier
physically.
Fight record: 2 wins, 2 ass kickins', 1 draw.
Psychologically, I'm 0 and 5;
I hated fighting.

TEARS ARE PROOF THAT YOU ARE REAL.

If you don't like "John Wayne Man,"
keep thinking
the way you do and maybe someone
you love will
commit suicide.

ODE TO THE BIG FISH

I scare so easily
I'd be easy to defeat
If we happen to meet angrily
Somewhere out on the street

Just say BOO!
And I'll run like the wind
I like to be gone
Before the trouble begins

But be careful who you terrorize
They may be different than me
You might just hook a big one
And be dragged into the sea

BULLY BIGOT RACIST PORN

Sissy, bitch, punk, *pussy*, *crybaby*,
girlboy, **nigga**, s p i c, *KIKE*,
JEW BASTARD, s a n d n i g g a, *fag*,
SLANT EYE, b e a n e r, **c o o n,**
CAMEL JOCKEY, d a g o,
c r a c ka, *guinea*, JEWBOY, CHINK,
j i g a b o o, cunt, **raghead,**
Fat Boy, WHITE TRASH,
j u n g l e b u n n y, TOWEL HEAD,
tar baby, HYMIE, *wap*

EXHALE HEAVILY

LGBTQW

Years ago I had a gay friend
who was like a brother to me.

He died of AIDS.

He said,
"You know, at least I have a
community for support.
Wimps don't even get a parade."
My response was,
"Thank you for noticing.
I can't even commit suicide,
I'm a Wimp."

We laughed.

DEPRESSION

**is not a sign of weakness.
It is a sign of being**

too strong for
too long.

My mind has caused me
a lot of trouble
during my lifetime.
I've tried losing it
on more than one occasion
but it keeps
finding its way back.

-

KC

*"There's something liberating about
public humiliation."*

Joaquin Phoenix

```
I rarely try to save face.
I usually just completely
    humiliate myself.
```

K̄C

99% of us are afraid of something.
The other 1% are freaks.

K̄C

All courage is not good.
Think perpetrators of the
Twin Towers.

K̄C

"The Hot"

There was that time in life
when I was "The Hot"
people were jealous
of all that I got

I didn't deserve it they said,
"The Hot" you are not
I'm glad it wasn't them
who decided "The Hot"

They line up to see you
when you got "The Hot"
even if you know
it's something you're not

"The Hot" seemed so confident,
so secure and complete
that's why it seems so strange
to see "The Hot" on the street

Seems "The Hot"
has cooled off,
the confidence subsided
looks like all the praise of
"The Hot"
was totally misguided

There was that time in life
when I was
"The Hot"

Easy Money

Easy Money
that's what I really want
Sleazy Money
the kind that you can flaunt

don't want to work
to eke out a meager livin'
want **Easy Money**
the kind that you are given

don't want to spend my time
slavin' away my day
don't want to do nuthin'
just wanna collect the pay

Easy Money
that's all I really want
Sleazy Money
the kind that you can flaunt

now ethics don't come into this
it's the state of mind I'm in
want **Easy Money**
every bet I make I win

Easy Money
that's what I really want
Sleazy Money
the kind that you can flaunt

House Full of Weirdos

I went to a house full of weirdos
weirdos were everywhere
I walked from one weird room to another
just breathing in all the weird air

I talked to weirdos along the way
to see if they had weird things to say
they did
yes, they did
they did
yes, they did

I met a weird woman
who had a weird kid
I tried to figure out what she was sayin'
but I never did

A weird guy came up to me
I said, "Please can you help me
figure it out."
He said, "It's just another form of prayin',
you just don't move your mouth."
I went to a

House Full of Weirdos

Writer's Block

I'll write tomorrow
but not tonite

I'll write tomorrow
when the feeling's right

I'll write right now
I've changed my mind

I can do it you know
I do it all the time

I'll write tomorrow
no, that'll be too late

I'll write tonite
now I can't wait

This writing about not writing
is writing alright

and it's plain to see
that I'm writing tonite

My Mind

Some people can memorize.
And because they can memorize,
they are considered smart.
I always had trouble memorizing
because you had to sit still and focus.

MY MIND IS
LIKE A
JAZZ BAND

that never stops playing until I fall asleep.

RUGGED INDIVIDUAL

WE ALL LIKE TO THINK
OF OURSELVES AS
INDIVIDUALS.

I KNOW I DO.

BUT THE FACTS
TELL A DIFFERENT STORY.

WE ARE ALL COMPOSITES.
THERE REALLY ARE
NO INDIVIDUALS.

ONLY COMPOSITES OF DNA AND
CIRCUMSTANCE.

ANYTHING ELSE IS
WISHFUL THINKING,
EGO OR BOTH.

BRAIN MAIL

First came Black Mail.
Then came Snail Mail.
Then Voicemail.
Later it was Email.
but it's really BRAIN MAIL
that's been around
the longest.
BRAIN MAIL: the answers
that come in the night to
questions from the day
before or longer. They just
show up while sleeping,
like mail.

BRAIN MAIL

The Equality of Bad

the bad Muslims
the bad cops
the bad parents
the bad siblings
the bad politicians
the bad dogs
the bad weather
the bad laws
the bad teachers
the bad priests
the bad whites
the bad blacks
the bad Chinese
the bad Fucking Russians
the bad Motherfuckers
the bad asses

The Bad

URBANITE

THERE AIN'T NUTHIN' LIKE A CITY
ON A COLD HOT RAINY DAY
YOU CAN SMELL THE LONELY PEOPLE
AS THEY THROW THEIR LIVES AWAY

DON'T TELL ME 'BOUT THE ROCKIES
OR THE DESERTS' SUNSETS BRIGHT
THERE AIN'T NUTHIN' LIKE A CITY
ON A COLD HOT SUMMERS NIGHT

YOU CAN MEET SO MANY PEOPLE
AS THEY WANDER AIMLESSLY
YOU CAN STOP AND TALK TO STREET LIGHTS
BUT THEY DON'T HAVE MUCH TO SAY

WHEN YOU START TO GET THE PICTURE
OF WHAT IT'S REALLY ALL ABOUT
IT'S NOT JUST BROKEN BUILDINGS
WITH THE WINDOWS ALL KNOCKED OUT

THERE AIN'T NUTHIN' LIKE A CITY
PUDDLED SIDEWALKS, RAINY DAYS
AND THE COLORS ARE NOT PRETTY
DIRTY, DINGY, BLACKS AND GRAYS

BUT IF YOUR FEELIN' PITY
FOR THE DIRT, WASTE AND NEGLECT
THERE AIN'T NUTHIN' LIKE A CITY
TO HELP YOU SOON FORGET

PEOPLE

I've lived in 24 or more cities
in my almost 70 years on Earth.
Here's what I saw:

PEOPLE are **RACIST** in every city

PEOPLE are **STRUGGLING** in every city

PEOPLE are **HAPPY** in every city

PEOPLE are **SCARED** in every city

PEOPLE are **THE SAME** in every city

PEOPLE are **DIFFERENT** in every city

PEOPLE are **TO BLAME** in every city

PEOPLE are **NOT TO BLAME** in every city

PEOPLE are PEOPLE in every city

Sorry?

Inner thoughts on the outside
That's just who I am

I'd like to say I'm sorry ma'am
But I don't give a good goddamn

No, I can't hide it
Though I've tried and tried

It just always seems to come out

The inside on the outside

The small talk *just got* big

The conversation just ended

I'd like to say I'm sorry ma'am
But I don't give a good goddam

The Philosophy of NO

NO Drinking
NO Smoking
NO Fisticuffs
NO High Fives
NO Selfies
NO Soulmates
NO Close Talkers
NO BFF's
NO Mean People
NO Hightech
NO Trends
NO Fads
NO Tattoos
NO Piercings
NO Cares

NO Hunting
NO Fishing ⇨ Credit The
NO Nothing *3 STOOGES*
GO Home

American Dream

He started out poor
diggin' ditches
Got a little money
and lots of bitches

The American Dream
not achieved by all

This is the story of his
rise and fall

Pimpin' and dealin'
lyin' and stealin'
Working the streets like a satanic demon

He rose to the top
but ended a flop
Now he's in prison
pushin' a mop

I watched guys like this for many years in
the French Quarter. They all believed they
would never be caught but all that thinking
went for naught. But the fashion was
amazing, especially the hats.

The Voices

Bills– *Which ones to pay?*

Kids– *What will happen to them?*

Politics– *Who's telling the truth?*

Sex– *Who wants me?*

Sports– *Who won?*

Money– *Do I have enough?*

Insurance– *Why?*

Driving– *Where am I going?*

Schools– *How?*

The Planet– *How long?*

Can someone PLEASE

Quiet The Voices

For the Sake of Money

For the sake of Money   I've lived in the cold

For the sake of Money   I've humored the old

For the sake of Money   I kissed so much ass

For the sake of Money   cuz I needed the cash

For the sake of Money   I worked myself to death

For the sake of Money   No different from the rest

For the sake of Money   I lost love and all that mattered

For the sake of Money   My confidence was shattered

For the sake of Money   My children grew up lonely

For the sake of Money   They found out I was phony

For the sake of Money   That bought nothing really needed

For the sake of Money   Even my decency retreated

For the Sake of Money

Hey, what's this cost?

We paid the price for who we are.
We are not clerks or bartenders or salesmen.
We paid the price for who we'll be.

My wife
My friend
My partner
And me.
My inspiration
My life
My friend
My wife.

We paid the price so we can get paid.
We can cash that check
now that the money's been made.
We paid the price for who we are.
We are not clerks or bartenders or salesmen.
So when it's time to get in line
for check out time,
remember, we are not clerks or
bartenders or salesmen

We are
Writers,
Poets,
Painters And ...

A Creative Mind

**A creative mind is a mind that is not confined
by ALL the rules of society.**
This is not to say that a person who is creative by nature
has a given right to break ALL the rules set down by the
masses either.
Just try to understand
that for this reason, creative people will
on occasion, be **misunderstood.**
By nature, they have little salesmanship;
therefore, they can sometimes seem aloof or distant.
Their minds never stop long enough to be "charming."
They see things that others don't see.
They hear things that others don't hear.
They are more sensitive in many different ways,
physiologically different.
Just like a homosexual doesn't "choose" to be gay,
a creative person didn't "choose" his or her mindset;
they seem to have been born that way.
**Without these creative minds the world would not
grow. Some of them suffer as outcasts of "normal"
society** but they are willing to live on the streets or
starve because of their need to create. A creative
person would buy paint before food, a guitar string
before a soda.
If they are lucky, they find someone who is either
creative or understands the malady and supports it.
If they are unlucky, they may live a life of loneliness
which can sometimes lead to anger or depression.
It would also not be fair to judge the masses too harshly
either. They only see what "they" see and can't
understand the unseen world around them.

Core

By Second grade we're pretty
much who we're going to be.
Our personalities develop
and are stifled to fit in.
By fourth grade our core is set.
Different events will bend
and stretch that core
but it is who you are
for the rest of your life.
At least, it's that way with me.
Although we are taught to camouflage
our personalities to fit in,
they don't go away.

I AM

4th grade

Kenny!

Not Grown Up

I really do love children.
Especially someone else's kids.
But I had no time for such illusions,
with all of their growing up confusions.

It seems I am a loner,
in love from time to time.
Still searching for that perfect song,
still trying to make it rhyme.

No, not much time for children
or adolescent cares.
You see,

I'm still a child myself, in search of pony rides and fairs.

Most of us are not trained to live past 60

—

KC

❧ ❧ ❧ ❧ ❧ ❧ ❧

Don't want to live forever

I'm closing in on 70 and
nothing,
absolutely nothing,
makes me wish that I were younger.
Wait, you can **freeze the games** with your
remote when you go to the bathroom.
That's pretty special.

Long Life

You know I've been so many people,

I still recognize a few.
But there are so many things they did,
things that I would never do.

The hats I wore all had one reason,
the compensation needed to exist.

And when the money starts rollin' in,
it gets impossible to resist.

But now I've lived long enough
to come out the other side.

Yes, I like the person I've become
and the space where he resides.

what was

what was *LOVE* is HATE
what was *UP* is DOWN
what was *RIGHT* is WRONG

what was
what was

what was *BLACK* is *WHITE*
what was *DAY* is *NIGHT*
what was *OPEN* is *CLOSED*

what was
what was

what was *COOL* is *NOT COOL*
what was *HAPPY* is *SAD*
what was *ANGRY* is *GLAD*

what was
what was

what was has *CHANGED*
what was is *OVER*

what was
what was
what was

We the people

BLACK people
WHITE people
Hope I meet the right people

NIGHT people
DAY people

The always want to **PLAY** *people*
Those always **IN THE WAY** *people*

The people **UNDER THE STEEPLE** *people*
The people who **DON'T CARE** *about people*

The **PROFESSIONAL** *people*
The **LAY** *people*

The I don't care what they say people

The **PREQUEL** *people*
The **SEQUEL** *people*

The **CO-EQUAL** *people*
The **UNEQUAL** *people*

We the people

We all matter

Be Prepared

When socializing for the evening,
one should always carry a sack of
"good to see ya's."
But whatever you do,
don't forget to bring two
"Fuck You's,"
just in case.

⚜ ⚜ ⚜ ⚜ ⚜ ⚜ ⚜

With Age Comes Wisdom

One of my biggest mistakes in life was
thinking that
OTHERS
somehow had ALL the answers
to MY problems.
I thought all my
FRIENDS
were smarter than they turned out to be.

There were years in my life when I found
myself fitting in with the people
who don't fit in.

—
KC

Friends

Rarely do we end up with
any of the ones we started with.

K̄C

The best way to know someone
is to tell them the
truth.

K̄C

Seedy Side

there's a seedy side
    to horse racing
there's a seedy side
    to catering
there's a seedy side
    to politics
there's a seedy side
    in the bar and restaurant business
there's a seedy side
    to agriculture
there's a seedy side
    to hiring
there's a seedy side
    in the entertainment industry
there's a seedy side
    of religion
there's a seedy side
    to medicine
there's a seedy side
    to the justice system

there's a seedy side

No Slack

I'd like to start with a confession
I didn't make a great first impression

I know I won't be invited back

makes me wonder why
people no different than I
make judgments so quickly
and sometimes so strictly

behavior so dickly
bad day
no way
just get out of the way

better be careful what you say
you won't be invited back

'cause even though
I'm just like you

I ain't cuttin' you
no slack

COVID Nursing Home Blues

My friends are all dyin'.
I buried two just yesterday.

They said they got the COVID
and it wouldn't go away.

Now the undertakers car
is out front everyday.

I had said I'd never do it.
They won't be puttin' me away.

But my friends are all dyin'.
I buried two just yesterday.

Now they say that you can't visit.
They keep sending you away.

But my friends are all dyin'.
I buried two just yesterday.

Death

It's never too late
that's not the truth
it can be too late
and I've got proof

Death

I decided to wait
and wait and wait
found out in fact
I was too late
my friend had died

Death

Daddy

"I'd be pissed if it didn't happen to everybody."

—

Bert Champagne (on death)

Sadly, this is the only thing my father said that ever made sense to me.

Those J've Known

Some went crazy
Some died young
Some were lazy
Some were just plain dumb
A few did great things
Some just stayed home
Seems my lot in life
Was to roam
And roam alone

—

KC

Alcohol ic

Remove the alcohol
and there's still the
ic
I've spent more than 35 years working on the
ic
And there's still plenty of
ic
to work on

The
Alcoholism/Recovery Part

First Day Sober October 9, 1983.
For the first time the world is Fucked up
and I'm not.

–

KC

Twelve Years of Mardi Gras

If you've ever been to **Mardi Gras,**
imagine **Mardi Gras** every night for twelve years.
From the age of 20-32 years old, my life was
equivalent to twelve years of **Mardi Gras.**
Pretty much seven nights and days a week for
twelve years.
The Real Mardi Gras.
The puking and the peed pants,
the cops and the sirens,
twelve years of **The Real Mardi Gras.**
The SEX in parked cars,
the SEX on the bar,
the SEX on the street,
the SEX in the ladies room,
the SEX in the game room,
the SEX with a girl from Missouri,
the SEX with a girl from Wisconsin,
the SEX with a girl from Detroit.
One girl from Italy even demanded SEX.
The Real Mardi Gras,
for twelve years.
The fights and the injured,
the "new" relationships,
twelve years of "new" relationships.
Their puke and peed pants.
Every night and day for twelve years.
The Real Mardi Gras.

Many died.
I'm not sure why I didn't.
I honestly have no idea why I survived.

ADDICTED

Yes it's true that I'm AFFLICTED
'cause you know that I'm ADDICTED
get HOOKED
on most anything I do

although I've kicked a few before
there's some that just WANT MORE
and sometimes
MORE is what I like to do

I DRINK too much
and SMOKE a lot
but I'm NEVER SATISFIED
with what I got

I'm ADDICTED
I'm ADDICTED

now when it comes to WOMEN
there's been more than a few
think it's time I admit it
I'm ADDICTED to YOU

I'm ADDICTED
I'm ADDICTED

SOCIAL ANXIETY

SOCIAL ANXIETY
>It's with me everyday

SOCIAL ANXIETY
>corrupts the things I say

SOCIAL ANXIETY
>I feel it standing next to you

SOCIAL ANXIETY
>seems like there's nothing I can do

SOCIAL ANXIETY
>makes me tremble and shake

SOCIAL ANXIETY
>everything I say is a mistake

SOCIAL ANXIETY
>I just want to be alone

SOCIAL ANXIETY
>can't even talk on the phone

SOCIAL ANXIETY
>it's so misunderstood

SOCIAL ANXIETY
>we'd change it if we could

SOCIAL ANXIETY

Better

took me a long time
til I knew better
took me a long time
'til I got it right
took me a long time
but I'm doin' better

in fact,
I'm doin' much better tonight

Achieving sobriety was not easy
but definitely worth the trouble

—
KC

My best friend told me he'd rather die
than go to AA
We buried him two years later

The Natural
"I believe we have two lives.
The one we learn with
and the one we live with afterwards."

Glenn Close from "The Natural"

Bad Information

All of my life people have been telling

me that I should act, " like a man."

I ignore them.

You ever notice the way men act?

Adding Insult To Injury

When I was a drunk,
I insulted people who
didn't deserve it.

When I got sober,
I insulted people
who did deserve it.

I remember a young woman came up
to me when I was tending bar in
Boulder, Colorado and said,
"You're an asshole."
And I said,
"I see we've met before
but you'll have to get in line
to hate me."

Recovery

What will be my contribution?
I have to make a resolution.
To live alone's not retribution
for the things that I have done.

For I have **taken.**
I have **needed.**
I forced my **love**
and then **retreated.**

What can I do
to make amends
to those I have mistreated?

If I isolate and I don't **repay,**
this new life given me **today,**
I'm told that it will go away.

What will I do to **start anew**
and break through my disguise?
I'll get involved from **day to day**
and stop telling so many lies.

Stay sober and **be kind.**
Make my phone an open line.
Be available from time to time.
Consider other lives, not just mine.

Transition

I was offered a job outside
the bar and restaurant business
and discussed the prospect at an AA meeting
in Stamford, CT, during my early
years of sobriety.

It would've been my first job outside
of the bar and restaurant business.

After the meeting, an "old timer" came up to me
and said the following:

"Ken, it's all shit."

You have two choices in life:

1. You can stand knee deep in it and shovel it into
   bags.

   Or
2. You can drive around in a fancy car, take orders
   and sell it by the truck load.

I took the sales job.

BANNED

DURING MY DRINKING YEARS,
I WAS BANNED FROM SO MANY PLACES
THAT I CAME TO BELIEVE THAT
I WOULDN'T DIE BUT
RATHER I WOULD BE BANNED FROM EARTH.

Please Don't Feed the Animals

Do you miss the clown show
now that he's gone
those footprints on the ceiling
the peeing on the lawn

you helped to feed the monkey
even when he tried to escape
but you'd disappear at closing time
leaving the monkey without his cape

you know you propped him up
for entertainment's sake
I hope you see
as he finally did
and admit

The Big Mistake

138

It's a Choice

So many people **go back**
They make a choice
then find they can't hack

So many people **go back**

So realize the power of **crack**

So many people **go back**

It'll make you think that

Jill is Jack

The ones who make it
choose not to take it

So many people **go back**

There's over 50 years of unindoctrinated
wisdom in this book. You can read it and grow
or you can bring it
to your church's book burning.
All I can do is try

Show me

Prove me wrong about anything
I've written in this book and I'll apologize.

Sometimes I didn't choose my experiences,
they chose me.

The Race
Seems the race was contested
In fact, Some of us got arrested
The riot squad was working overtime
I stood back and watched the melee
And although I really wanted to stay
I ran just like the rest of you did

**None of the following letters have helped
to keep my two nieces sober but you have to try.**

Dear C G,   Sometime in 2010
*I don't pretend to know how hard your battle will be or
how tough anyone's will be but I've never forgotten how
hard mine was. I tried it my way over and over with
sincerity and determination and I continually went back
to drinking.*
*Only when I became humble and realized I had one last
chance did I start to get well. I mean it. I had lost jobs
and friends that would never be regained, gone forever.
Good jobs, good friends, run off by my alcoholism.
Relationships destroyed forever.*
*Only after I got a sponsor and did what was suggested
did I start to really recover. I had a good no nonsense
sponsor who had me making coffee for a month, told me
to go shake hands and thank every speaker and told me
that AA wasn't a dating service but rather a life
changing experience.*
*I didn't always like his suggestions but they worked and I
didn't drink. That's what I was there for and it worked.
Pretty much everything he said would happen,
happened, he was uncanny. I asked him how he knew
and his answer was that when you boil us down we're
all the same. Rich, poor, male, female, powerful heads of
corporations or street sweepers; we're all drunks.*
*After 27 years sober you'd think I'd feel cured. I know
from others that I'm not cured, but rather in remission,
contingent upon one thing. DON'T INGEST ALCOHOL.
I hope to continue in remission until I'm at least 80. I
may drink when I'm 80, I'm thinking Hennessey and
lime over ice. Yes, if I live 21 more years I may drink but
I'm not drinking today. That I'm sure of.*
Uncle Kenny and Aunt Bobbi,
Our dog Spirit is also in recovery from desertion
We are all very supportive of each other.

And try...

C G, 3/1/11

You'd think I'd have something better to do than to write this short letter. Especially since I haven't heard back after sending that wonderful decaf coffee and chicory. What a concept, decaf coffee. Seems like an oxymoron.

Charlie Fuckin' Sheen! That's why I'm writing. Each of us has the right to draw the lines that we won't cross or think we won't cross in regards to our personal beliefs. I try not to tell anyone where to draw their lines and I refuse to let anyone tell me where my line should be drawn, with the exception of someone with a loaded gun.

Charlie Fuckin' Sheen reminds me so much of my deceased best friend Joey. I will always remember the day he told me, "I'd rather die than go to A.A."

I probably mentioned him in my first letter to you. If I did mention my friend, I also mentioned that I buried him two years later. You see, he drew his line and I drew mine. I'm typing this letter and he never lived to see his children grow up.

So, I'll not judge Charlie Fuckin' Sheen. It's his right to draw his own line. And it is true that the A.A. life was sometimes very boring but at least I lived to write this letter.

KC

And try…

Dear C G,   *Jan 2020*

*We hurt a lot of people, don't we, when we're doing what
we do. I hurt a lot of people but blamed them. Some folks
forgave me. Some folks will never forgive me and there
are a few who probably still want me dead.*

*I discovered that everyone has a different timetable for
forgiveness and that I had to live with the consequences
of my actions. Until I understood exactly how bad I had
hurt others, I could never get well. I quit hanging around
with my drinking and drugging friends. It wasn't a lot of
fun but it was necessary. They're all dead, gone too
soon. What a waste.*

*As I've stated before, I just started doing what I was told
to do and it worked. Eventually, things got better.*

*I'm still fucking crazy but I quit doing the things that got
me in trouble, especially with the law. I even quit
speeding. You see, if you're mentally different, they will
lock you up. I'd rather be crazy and free rather than
crazy and incarcerated.*

*Although I haven't seen you since you were very little, I
know you and I know how you think because I know
addicts and when you boil us down we're all the same.
Part of my experience was blaming others. It was always
their fault.*

*Nothing I did was repaired overnight. I was told to take
it slow, make no demands and remember, it is your
actions that govern how you are perceived. It took me a
while but I finally got it. Hope you can, too. We all have
a choice until our actions give others jurisdiction over
our lives. I hope you don't lose your freedom or worse,
your life. Uncle Kenny*

And try…

There are those who think that because they
don't see the pain they cause,
they can deny causing it.
I was once one of those people.
Ya' know, "If a tree falls in the woods…

$\overline{KC}$

Dear C G,   *Feb 2020*
*All I can tell you is what I did. I stopped listening
to myself and just started doing what my sponsor
told me. I read a lot. I went to 3 meetings a day for
7 years on my own and I needed every one. No one
checked on me. I changed all of my "friends." By
the way, all my "friends" are dead. They left behind
great sadness before and after they died. No one
made me get sober. No one makes me do anything.
Well, maybe if they have a gun or a pit bull.*
   *It's your life. A lot of people get clean and stay
clean. It really is a personal choice. You can't get
addicted to something you don't ingest.*
Best,
Uncle Kenny
*P.S. I am not well, so this is really all I have. It's
your choice anyway. It really is your choice.*

And try…

Dear Legal Niece S,   *May 2020*

I try not to make judgments about people based on what I hear, especially about someone I've never met. But I remember my experimental years and the destruction and pain those "experiments" caused me and others.

First off, I didn't do any experimenting while living with my parents. What you are doing to your parents is cruel. My parents knew very little about the life I led in my 20's. It would've killed them. It almost killed me.

When my experimenting 20's were over, I was an alcoholic, sex addict, drug addict, unemployed, depressed and mostly disliked person by anyone who knew me. I also had acquired a long list of venereal diseases. It took 20 more years of hard work and pain to recover from my alcoholism.

I finally started listening to other people, successful and happy people. Two feelings that had escaped me. But then I actually reprogrammed my brain somewhat. I discovered "modeling." Modeling my behavior to that of someone who seemed happy and content instead of dirt balls.

It took a long time but I didn't quit and now I'm married to your aunt. Sometimes that fact alone makes me wish I was still drinking- just kidding. I realized that life is hard enough without me fucking it up even more.

KC Wishing you the best.

One last reminder: the deeper the hole, the longer it will take to get out and sadly some don't get out. I buried a lot of friends in my 20's. What a waste.

145

Note to my Wife

That's not your niece
that's not the little girl you knew

that's a drug addict
I sat next to her for years

she will be a drug addict
until she chooses not to be one

she will steal
she will lie

all the ones I sat next to are dead
the ones that didn't stop

she will be a drug addict
until she decides not to be one

she will hurt herself
and everyone who loves her

she can make her life a dream
or a nightmare

she will be a drug addict
until she decides not to be one

Remembering

What came before
was life for sure
but life worth living
it was not
Mistakes that were made
drunk or stoned I can't trade
for desires and dreams I have not

but the truth of it is
and I just couldn't resist
the mistakes are the past
but I'm not

for you see, I'm today
and it's really okay
to remember
the things you forgot

Sex, Love and Broken Hearts

"Not a better feeling in the world to a man
than to be approaching his own doorstep
knowing that someone is on the other side
listening for his footsteps."

—

Clark Gable

American Logic

I've always found it odd
that watching two people
pleasure each other is against the law,
while watching two people
beating the crap out of each other
is legal.

—

KC

OH MY GOD!

Although it was many,
many years ago,
I will always
remember/never forget
when my
condom covered penis
entered a vagina
for the first time.

OH MY GOD!

"Females make males stupid and crazy"
—

Ron Magill, Zoo Miami

MOST POWERFUL DRUG ON EARTH

Why?

Do Men Throw Everything Away For It?

Is it Heroin?

Is it Cocaine?

POWERFUL Men, SUCCESSFUL Men

Why?

Bill Clinton, Tavis Smiley, Matt Lauer, Charlie Rose, that Governor from South Carolina, etc

Heads Of Companies

Why?

Because It's The Most Powerful Drug

On Earth

A VAGINA

If you wonder why men want
SEX ALL THE TIME,
you haven't had the pleasure
of placing your
ERECT PENIS
inside of a
HOT WET VAGINA.
If you had, you wouldn't wonder.

$\overline{KC}$

Seventies Sex

There was so much sex in the 70's,
that on more than one occasion,
everyone I knew was fucking
everyone I knew.

I personally had so much sex in
the 70's, I actually woke up one
morning with my dick laying next to
me. He was gasping for breath. I
asked him if he was ok and he said,
"Can we please just stop for a
while? Can you just give it a rest? "

And yes, my penis talks. All men's
penises speak to them from
puberty until death.

Dating Service Advertising

G Harmony

females are perfect

perfect teeth

perfect breasts

don't have periods

poop once a month

while you're at the game

G Harmony- Sign up today!

New Love

If I could have my choice
of anywhere I'd be
it would be alive and well
with you right next to me

yes, it could be a city
with lights and sounds unique
or it could be wide open land
with barns and harvests sweet

or floating down a river
waters rushing by
in the middle of a forest
where weeping willows cry

or sailing on the ocean
or flying in some sky
in the quiet of a desert
or a train station's hellos and goodbyes

yes, up above the clouds
or deep below the sea
it wouldn't matter where it was
if you were there with me

Head and Heart

I looked here and I looked there
I couldn't find her anywhere
except inside my Head and Heart

my head is tormenting me
my heart won't let me see
that in fact it's not up to me

it's really up to my Head and Heart

so I got back in my car and drove uptown
but everyone said they hadn't seen her around

maybe she was only in my Head and Heart

they said I should've known it from the start
they say I should've used my head
and not my heart

red flags they said
popped up in the first inning
you should've seen this coming
from the very beginning

my head is tormenting me
my heart won't let me see
that in fact it's not up to me

it's really up to my Head and Heart

First Date

Can I take you out to dinner?
Would you walk with me tonight?
Can I smile and have you
take my arm,
then hold my hand real tight?

Can we have light conversation?
Can we say everything just right?
Would you kiss me on a street corner,
underneath a city light?

And when the night is over
and I awaken from my dream,
be gentle with reality,
'cause it's never what it seems.

storeroom love

where to go? what to do?
you want me and I want you
but it's the middle of the day.
an eight hour day
twenty minute breaks, so let's break away

storeroom love
on the shelves up above
new styles, old fads
they won't get in our way

storeroom love
gotta get 'em off quick
don't fold your clothes
hurry, quick, quick, quick

storeroom love
puts a smile on your face
I hear someone's coming
better straighten up this place
and brush your hair
hey, do you see my underwear?

back to work now
but oh my, my
lunch time love

put a twinkle in my eye

Balance

I was a bartender

from the age of 20 to 32,
most of that time in
New Orleans.
During that time,

I had more sex than should be humanly possible.

It was the 70's and AIDS wasn't a thing
yet. And back then women were even
into it. Really into it.
Then I got sober, cured of my
venereal diseases and I got a job as a
manufacturers rep, which is basically
on the road all week.
From the age of 32-50

I got less sex than should be humanly allowable.

I guess life is about

Balance.

Are DOUBLE STANDARDS OK
when fighting
DOUBLE STANDARDS?

If you don't want it to be about your looks,
then don't make it about your looks:

Lipstick (that makes your lips look wet)
High heels (that prop your ass up)
Tight skirts (you know what they do)
Long underwear (you call leggings)
Cleavage (especially talking cleavage).

What do you think that makes us think of?
If you wear a "come Fuck me" outfit,
I promise you, we will think of Fucking.

Sure, men should have to control themselves
but it should be about mutual respect,
especially at work.
Or should men walk around in skin tight
leggings bulging from all the
obvious places acting like,
"Whaaat?
Why are you staring at my bulge?
What's your problem?"

Plus, when you dress like that,
I don't hear a word you're saying.

Along these same lines, women who know better, should tell women who don't know better, that when dressing for work, sexy is not professional. Professional is professional. If you dress sexy, the outfit will get all of the attention.

Certainly, you have a right to dress as you choose. Personally, I like skin but this reminds me of my friend's son who had just cut his hair in a Mohawk and dyed it fire engine red. After a walk on Clearwater Beach, he returned to our group and was pissed that everyone was staring at him.

Believe the Cleave

One of my favorite things in life has always been

cleavage.

However, some women use it as a weapon. Some cleavage actually talks. I love watching men act like they don't notice a woman flaunting her tits, only to walk up to me and say,

"TITS!"

Girlfriend

It's Friday now
she deserves some fun
some good times
she will have

But not too late
or she'll seal her fate
'cause her week
is not yet done

Two jobs, that's what she's got
the one she's workin'
and the one she's not

Yes, she'll rush to wake up
and put on makeup
then hurry to open the store

Now when Sunday is done
and the new week begun
she prepares to do it
once more

I Married for Money

I don't care about regular people
they don't exist anymore in my life
you can say what you want
about the common man

but I made a wealthy woman my wife

now don't cop the wrong opinion
and don't think that I ruined my life
'cause it wasn't the woman I married
when I made a wealthy woman my wife

I married for money
can't lie
I married for money
don't try
I married for money
when I made a wealthy woman my wife

now I drive a real fancy car
and I'm known in most every bar
you know I spend a lot of money
'cause I've got a lot of money to spend

cont

I married for money
can't lie
I married for money
don't try
I married for money
when I made a wealthy woman my wife

By the way, I personally didn't marry for
money. It's just a poem. Relax

Indigestion

You know it really pains me
when you try to rearrange me
make me into something I am not

I tried to make a suggestion
instead I've got indigestion
and there's something that
you totally forgot

You really liked me when you met me
told me you would let me
be the guy who sweeps you off your feet

Well, I haven't really changed
I think it's you who've
rearranged
the furniture inside our lovely suite

DIVORCE

Somebody described DIVORCE to me this way:
You have a cow, the cow being your money. You put the man on one end of the cow and the woman on the other. Then you put the lawyers on two milking stools and let them go to work.

After almost three years of MILKING, from a three month long marriage, I developed a new appreciation for "lawyer jokes." I actually asked my first lawyer if before passing the bar exam you're required to leave your soul or was it voluntary?

I FIRED HER, THE INCOMPETENT BITCH.

Cost me ten grand to get a new lawyer. My big mistake was to tolerate her incompetence for close to three years.
Remember this was a three month long marriage and I'm not rich.

I also learned that there are really only two kinds of people, users and givers. My new goal is to meet a giver and out give her. I learned a lot of expensive and painful lessons BUT I LEARNED THEM and they are behind me now.

THE SAME MISTAKES WON'T BE MADE AGAIN.

Now that the DIVORCE is final, I have a new appreciation for little things. Each day without a lawyer in your life is a great day.

I'm also making a lot less money than I have in many years but I can't remember when I've been happier.
This seems to be the nature of life's highway. Sometimes it makes you feel like you're in a continuous construction zone but believe me there are smooth lanes up ahead.
Maneuver the potholes, drive softly over the bumps and survive. Come out the other end of the tunnel to where the sun is shining, glance occasionally in the rear view mirror but keep your eyes in front of you.
There's just too much ahead to keep looking back.

Honest Pick Up Line

Excuse me, I was wondering if I could move my
erect penis in and out of your vagina
at a rapid pace later on this evening?
She said yes.
(New Orleans 1972)

The Beauty of Life

I wonder if the people who find life so beautiful
would still feel the same if they were forced to
watch the act that procreated them while in
progress. If you think about it, life is pretty gross.
Don't think about it and
remember, they were young and back then they
did it in the dark.

I've always thought of myself as a byproduct
of sexual intercourse.

—

KC

No Reason

What if I liked you
for a year or so
or six months
or a week
or a night
who knows

would it hurt
would you cry
would it make you angry
would you live
would you die

what if you loved me
for a day
or a week
and left on a Thursday
without even a peep

what would I say
what would we do
if you stopped loving me
and I stopped loving you

Darkness

Did you ever sit in your room at night
and wish the phone would ring?

Have you ever walked through a beautiful
park and hated everything?

Well, lately I have felt this way
almost every day.

And I think I know the reason,
it's 'cause you've gone away.

If I could change what can't be changed,
I'd change it anyway.

If I could draw a picture
of all the things I've said,

I'd try to draw exactly
the thoughts inside my head.

But I can't draw and I don't paint
and I can't change a thing.

So I'll sit and wait
for those love letters that
the postman doesn't bring.

Liar

I can't blame it on the weather
'cause the sun is shinin' bright
but I wish it was a rainy day
followed by a rainy night

As my tears pour down like raindrops
cats and dogs would be surprised
it's the truth that makes me weep tonight

it's the truth
beneath your lies

I can't blame it on the weather
'cause the sun is shining bright
but the forecast is for cloudy days
and there's no relief in sight

People who HATE each other will still
FUCK

–

KC

fragile
heart

I must be gentle
I must be kind
I must move slowly

with this heart of mine

or did I forget 'cause I better remember
how easily it falls apart

this fragile heart

this fragile heart

so eager for giving
brought back from the dead
once again it is living

but I must be gentle
I must be kind
I must move slowly

with this heart of mine

I cannot risk at this stage of recovery

a heart so fragile

a heart so lovely
I must be gentle
I must be kind
I must move slowly

with this heart of mine

Too Late

I zipped through my life
without children or wife
and plenty of time to burn.
Well I burned it all up.
No one shares in my cup
but I'm left with these
lessons I've learned.

Things have changed since I wrote this.
    I hit the mammal lottery with my
wife and a year later we found a tiny
Cocker Spaniel puppy abandoned and
alone in a cemetery off a two lane
county road in Arkansas. She has been
with us for 14 years.
Maybe I should have called this,

Almost Too Late

In America
Religion has become just another way
to divide people,
as if racial divisions weren't enough.

KC

Fairness or Hypocrisy

I decided to write about how I feel about
religion in general, after
White Evangelicals gave us
d rump.
Religion has become weaponized and because
of this, I decided to speak my truth.
While my beliefs are in direct opposition
to the general public, so were the beliefs of
Jesus Christ at the time.
I hope you don't give me the same
disrespect that he received.

Big Surprise

I believe that the pompous, self righteous, coat and tie wearin', hymn singing, bible quotin' , Evangelicals are in for a "Big Surprise" when they get to the "Pearly Gates."

Saint Peter: Hi guys, welcome to the "Pearly Gates."

Let's see now, this looks great:

✔ church every Sunday all dressed up, that's a bonus

✔ brought cake to pot luck fundraisers, that's good

✔ great singer of hymns, nice

✔ oh wow - you could actually quote bible versus

✔ voted Republican

Wait a second, voted Republican?
Wait, I'm starting to see a problem
Yep, here it is
RACIST!

Sorry guys, you're in the wrong line.
The down elevator is to the right.
See the guy in the Red Suit.

Honest Liars

As soon as I realized that life was
temporary and religion was a scam,
it pissed me off.

I had been lied to
by everyone I trusted.

Although these people may have believed
what they told me,
as it turns out they were wrong.

They told me black people were less than.
They told me Jews were bastards.
They told me Mexicans were thieves.
And on and on.

I was fed these lies.

If you called them lies you were ostracized.

Child Abuse

I left home
at seventeen and a half years old
with a backpack and anger
as my only two possessions.

The backpack was one of many objects
I lost along the way.

The anger has never really
left completely.

It races to the top in times of:

hurt

–

sorrow

–

depression

–

guilt

–

and anxiety.

You know, the byproducts of
religious indoctrination.

A Secular Society

I learned over my lifetime that a person can make himself believe almost anything. But just because you believe it, doesn't make it true.

The Constitution gives religious people the right to believe what they believe. It doesn't give them the right to force others to believe what they believe.

This is America not Christianica.

For every example of

God's so-called love,

I can show you ten times as many examples of

God's lack of love.

I am convinced that humanity can do alot better without these absurd stories.

Indoctrinated

As you go through life
thinking your decisions are up to you
one day you will discover
others govern all you do

You've been *indoctrinated*

though you think it's up to you
there's really nothing that you do
that's really only you

You've been *indoctrinated*

that's right, you've been

Regulated
Segregated
Manipulated
Indoctrinated

and there's nothing you can do
'cause those who   you
were indoctrinated, too

GOOD MAN OF FAITH

While it would be wrong

to call me a

"GOOD MAN OF FAITH"

I'd have no problem

if you called me a

"GOOD MAN OF FACT"

because that's

what I have become

Religious faith is the height of
Narcissism

—

KC

JUST SOME OF THE "ONE TRUE" GODS

THE GREEKS (no longer exists)
THE ROMANS (no longer exists)
THE INCAS (no longer exists)
THE AZTECS (no longer exists)
THE MAYANS (no longer exists)
THE CHRISTIANS (all subsets)
THE JEWS (all subsets)
THE MUSLIMS (all subsets)
THE MORMONS
THE SIKHS
THE HUMANISTS
Almost forgot THE PAGAN'S

In a way, they all believe the same thing. That something unearthly is available when needed. But only if you worship it, burn something, give money, etc. As humanity became more enlightened, old beliefs were replaced by new beliefs but in name only because in a way, they all believe the same thing. I know firsthand from AA that the feeling of not being alone can be extremely powerful, it still doesn't mean that you are not alone.

50 years an adult

Religion changed in my lifetime from a spiritual experience to something similar to belonging to a club or a **gang**. In fact, some **religions** have become tax free **gangs**. Remember, way more money is stolen in a suit than in a hoodie.

After many years of searching, I no longer believe that any of the **religious** texts (Bible, Koran, Book of Mormon, etc.) are the direct word of a Creator/God.

While I do believe that Mary and Jesus existed, I do not believe in a virgin birth. I believe Mary was raped by a Roman soldier, which happened a lot back then and her parents knew that she would be blamed as a sinner for her own rape. Men were never wrong back then; women were possessions. In fact, I think **women were possessions until about 1972.** So anyway, this young girl, Mary, is all of a sudden pregnant. The real father we'll never know because we were taught this ridiculous story of a virgin birth. Mary's parents asked Joseph, a friend of the family, to get Mary out of town to spare her the punishment for her own rape. To me, this story just makes more sense and does nothing to diminish the wonderful teachings of Mary's son, Jesus.

I just cannot believe the barbaric stories in these old texts.

It's just hard for me to comprehend why an all knowing, all powerful God, would create everything with a defect (original sin) and then come to the conclusion that the best way to fix it would be to send his only son down to earth to be tortured and put to a violent death. No loving father would allow his only son to be butchered in this way if he had the power to stop it. Not to mention this unsuspecting young girl, Mary. What about Mary's feelings? Was Mary asked to carry this child? Was Mary as surprised as everyone else? Or are Mary's feelings not included in the story because it was written by MEN?

All powerful, all loving and then this bullshit.

I cannot make that leap of faith. For some reason, the real Creator, whatever it may turn out to be, (see Steven Hawking) could find a better way.

Moreover, Jesus said nothing about homosexuals or abortions. Saint Paul might have been a homophobe but not Jesus. If abortion and homosexuality were important to him, he would've said something.

Then, add to all of that, the amount of human hands and mouths that were used to dictate these stories and then write them down. Just too much to believe, too far-fetched, too judgemental, too bizarre. HALLUCINOGENS?

But I do believe in the teachings of Jesus as they relate to kindness and responsibility.

A God?
I just don't think so.

I've come to believe Stephen Hawking a lot more than the Vatican or any of the money makin' Megachurches of today, (see Joel Osteen and his co-pastor wife). How much tax free money do these smiling Motherfuckers make?

It has been my experience that a person doesn't necessarily have to believe in a Supreme Being to be a good human being.

180

Faith Based Initiative

At its best, religion can comfort and console. I believe these man-made religions based on the writings of humans with the same prejudices and bigotry of modern humans, at their worst, can be deadly.

Remember, 911 was a "faith-based initiative." Suicide bombings are "faith-based initiatives." Murdering doctors who perform abortions are "faith-based initiatives."

I'm leaning towards believing that science itself is God. That it's an abstract.

But it's certainly not an old bearded white guy up in the sky.

Read Steven Hawking's book, "A Brief History of Time." And remember, these mega church preachers, who prey on the ignorant and in some cases, even convinced the educated, are making more money than college football coaches. Man, that's a lot of doe.

September 2001

Where was God on 9/11?
and where was his
begotten son?

Was there something they could've done?

or did they create us just for fun?

Where was God on 9/11?

They watched the madness
from up above
while we were taught
that they were love

Where was God on 9/11?

Would you rather
live next to an honest, kind,
respectful neighbor
who didn't believe in God
or a religious fanatic?

‾
KC

The Sermon at the Border Wall

And d rump said:

Put the kids in cages
take the babies from their mothers
and scare them both to death
arrest the homeless
kill the buffalo so the native people
starve
put blacks in chains and enslave them
cheat on your wife when she's pregnant
and lie about it
vote Republican- double the vote of a
neo-Nazi
teach hate if it helps you win
'cause winning is everything
open a charity and use it for yourself
open a bogus school
don't pay people who've done work
for you
claim bankruptcy

*And All The Followers Did
What d rump said!*

Now is Not the Time

Don't pray for me
just let me be
your thoughts and prayers
are wasted on me
I don't believe the stories you tell
I don't believe in Heaven or Hell
Don't pray for me
just let me be
your empty words don't matter to me
By the way, when exactly is the time
To Talk About It?

⚜ ⚜ ⚜ ⚜ ⚜ ⚜ ⚜

Heaven or Hell

I've believed for many years that
Heaven and Hell
are not places we are transported to at death.
Heaven and Hell
like most of the stories in the Bible, are metaphors
for how we lived our lives.
If our lives were righteous,
Heaven
is a place where we already live.
If we were dirtballs, our lives were inevitably
Hell
and so to our eternity.

The Second Thing

First we are toilet trained.
The second thing
we are taught as children is
To Judge Others.
That is where *racism* and *bigotry* begins.

It is *delivered sometimes subtly, sometimes directly,*
by our *parents, grandparents, neighbors, friends, etc.*
It's so hard, if not impossible, not to join in
when you're young.
Some of us point *fingers and judge harshly,*
even later in life.

Childhood sticks to us unless we take
steps to remove it.

The One True Religions

If I were a Jew
I know what I'd do
I'd do what I like, pay no attention to you

but I was raised Catholic
the religion that's right
it helps me to sleep when I'm in bed at night

now, what about Buddhists
well aren't they a trip
oriental religions? No, I think I'll skip

Protestants, Lutherans, and Latter Day Saints,
got nuthin' on Babdists
'cause they think they're great

Now, you've all heard of Muslims
Sikhs and the like
Episcopal Ministers who play in the night

but give me the Catholics
that water and wine
yeah, that guilt filled religion to mess with my mind

now if your religion
gives you peace of mind
keep prayin' to your God but I'm doin' just fine

Raised a Catholic

Born and raised a Catholic. Catholic school
from first grade through twelve. Two of those
years were in a seminary studying to be a
Catholic priest. These were my parents' and
grandparents' beliefs. They became my
beliefs, for a while.
Until they became unbelievable....

Jesus
God
Yaweh
Holy Ghost
Holy Spirit
Saints
Virgins
Arch Angels
Regular Angels
Cherubs
SINS SINS SINS
Venial Sins
Mortal Sins
Confession
Holy Water

Knowing what we know now, confessing to a man in a long black gown behind a screen, in the dark, seems pretty weird. I went to confession every Saturday as a little boy. As I got older, I went less and less until I stopped going all together.

Holy water, the same guy in the black gown waves his hand over it and it becomes Holy. What a concept. I would've liked to have been at the business meetings where these concepts were first discussed. I can imagine how the conversations must've gone;
"Now, let's see, you're telling me we're gonna convince regular people that
'eat my body, drink my blood'
is a good idea?
We'll have to promise them Heaven.
Now, you're thinkin'...."

Mustn't forget Novenas:
Special prayers you pay for.
By the way,
you pay for everything.
Ask for the price sheets
Varies per Parish

I won't be able to WHAT?

I was raised so Catholic that
I spent two years in the seminary
studying to be a Catholic priest.
During that time,
the reality of celibacy set in,
ending my desire to be a Catholic priest.

Good Catholic Boy

When I was young, I was an altar boy.
One of my jobs was to service the Holy
water dispensers in the church.
I'll never forget the day I saw mosquito
larvae swimming in the Holy water
and I said to my 9 year old self,
"That can't be good."
Then I thought,
"At least they're 'Blessed'."

Preaching Division

My biggest problem with all religions is that they teach their children that they are better than those who disagree with the particular mythology that the parents want their children to believe.

I grew up as a Catholic. I was taught that it was a sin to go into a Jewish synagogue or any other place of worship that wasn't of my own faith.

That's real love isn't it? Teaching your children that those who don't believe the mythology that you believe aren't loved equally by God. These same religious people also told us that white kids and white people in general were superior in God's eyes. What an evil thing to teach to children.

For some reason I saw through racism by the age of twelve. The rejection of all religions was to take many, many more painful years.

This reminds me of a story my wife told me about the old Catholic tradition of not eating meat on Fridays. My wife, who was also raised Catholic, was shuttled to Catechism every Wednesday in grammar school. One Friday at lunch in the cafeteria, one of her co-Catechismers was about to eat a hamburger, when my 5th grade wife verbally accosted her 5th grade friend with,
"You can't eat that! It's Friday!"
Her friend, immediately looked at my 5th grade wife and said what amounted to the 5th grade version of, *"Go Fuck Yourself."*
Indoctrination at its finest! They haven't spoken since.

Just Close Both Your Eyes

I believe in goodness
but I don't believe in God
Now I realize that to some of you
that might seem a little odd

The stories in the books so strange
the miracles and the locust plagues
Two testaments that disagree
just exactly what God should be

Is God angry and vengeful?
Will God be kind to you and me?
I looked at both the books
and they just kept confusing me

Then I stepped back to look at the others
Koran, Book of Mormon just to name a few
I went to 15 different worship places
over a year or two
to see what they were preaching
to see exactly what they knew

Cont.

All of our mothers told us to
believe what they preached
but some of our mothers
had different beliefs
they passed them down
and no proof did they seek

but as I got older
and finished my study
the clarity I'd sought
had actually turned muddy

some teachings were common sense
don't need no God to think of that
then the stories get crazy
virgin births and things like that

So here's what I decided
about what happens when you die
you won't know it when it happens

You Just Close Both Your Eyes

My Religious Friends

The things you believe are the
direct opposite of the natural world.
  1. Virgin Birth (Rape)
  2. Bring back the dead (Coma)
  3. Walk on water (Sandbar)
Remember these folks believed the world was
flat.

You believe these things because:
  1. Your mom and dad taught you
  2. Everyone in your area believes the same
  3. They make you feel better

  These beliefs help you deal with the ugliness of
life.
But that still doesn't make them true.

  It's not fair for you, a religious person, to say
that I'm attacking your religion because I've read
the same material and came to a different
conclusion.

Life is not as simple as:

"Jesus Said"
or
"Just Say No."

I've learned over the past 50 years that
life is definitely not black or white
but rather multi-layered and many shades of color.

193

Born Again Friend

I was riding with a "born again" friend of mine,
I think he's a Pentecostal or something like that,
when he said to me, "You have more Christian
values than a lot of the members of my church.
Why don't you call yourself a Christian?"

I don't remember my answer but this is what I
wish my answer would've been:

Because of the atrocities and the arrogance.
Because of the lies I was told since childhood.
Because of the atrocities white Christians
committed against the natives. You know, the
fact that we stole their land and killed their
people. Because we enslaved Africans for free
labor and because of all the hypocrisy.

Plus, America did to religion what it did to pizza,
bastardized it, monetized it and then weaponized
it.

I also have a problem with the embellishments
of Jesus' accomplishments in the New Testament.
I do not believe that a God of any kind has ever
walked this planet, except maybe Shaq. No wait,
he's a Genie.

There are so many human fingerprints all over
the Bible, that I see a lot of the stories as no
different from Paul Bunyon or John Henry.
Folklore.

I'm offended when "good" is equated with
believing the stories in the Bible and being able
to "quote the verses."

By the Grace of God

Beliefs are directly related
to the life experiences one has had.

What your mother and father believed
has a lot to do with
what you believe even later in life.

Although I once prayed,
I no longer do so and haven't for over 25 years.

Nothing I have achieved
in the last 25 years is the result of prayer
of any kind.

It is the result of
being ready when luck came my way.

I no longer need the fantasy of religion or God.
That doesn't mean I accomplished it alone.

But it wasn't by the Grace of any God.

The Influence of the Buddha

It is said
that Jesus was exposed to the teachings of the
Buddha and in fact, that is how he
came to teach

peace, love and responsibility for others.

Had he not traveled,
he quite likely would not have been crucified.

What he preached
was in conflict with the government
at the time.
Thus,
he was persecuted and eventually murdered.
Similar to what would happen to him today.

—

(see David Koresh)

God's Reasons

Tell me about God
Won't someone tell me about God
It's so easy to believe sometimes
It's so easy to believe

But what about the hungry, the sick and those
without a home
Tell THEM about God
Won't someone tell THEM about God
It's impossible to believe sometimes
It's impossible to believe

But what about recoveries from terminal disease
The alcoholic who no longer has to drink
or the addicts drug- free release
It's so easy to believe sometimes
It's so easy to believe

I hope this God has reasons
for letting us exist
If I thought I had the power
I'd probably insist
Tell me about God
Won't someone tell me about God

Sanity City

Put two towns together from scratch.
The first town has people who are educated
but not religious.
The second town is all religious people
but not the same religion.
Knowing what you know,
which town do you think would survive
the longest?

By the Grace of my Wife

I've had a lot of medical issues over the last
couple of years and I never asked
God for help.

My wife and I got through it.

Now, if I had prayed, I would believe that
God helped me through it.

But it was my wife.

I am an alcoholic and sober for 35 years.
Most alcoholics say, *"By The Grace of God."*
I no longer say that because I'm sober because
I don't drink.
Not by the grace of God
but with the help of many other alcoholics.
I don't pray but if you think it helps you,
by all means, pray.

Identity Theft

The teachings of Jesus
have been
discarded
but his

brand
is being exploited for

❧ ❧ ❧ ❧ ❧ ❧ ❧

The List

How ironic that the political party with the least Christ-like policies have the majority of the White Evangelical Christian vote. Don't take my word for it. Below is the full list of Christ-like policies in the Republican Party:

1)...

The Atrocities

I believe the majority of religious people are well meaning. If Christians lived like Christ did, I might call myself a Christian but *Christians are taught that we are better than non-Christians.*
And let's be honest.
It was white Christians who bought and sold slaves.
It was white Christians that voted for the Jim Crow laws.
It was white Christians who blew up Oklahoma City.
And remember most of the mass murderers in the US are white Christian men.
A friend of mine once told me this country was built on Christian values.
I asked him,

"When did slavery become a Christian value?"

Coincidentally, that was over fifteen years ago and was also the last time we spoke.

FILLING THE JAILS

Saying that a woman who has an abortion is a murderer, is like calling the general who orders draftees to storm the beach, a murderer.

Both made their decisions based on what they believed is better for mankind and society as a whole. And remember, the draftees, just like the fetus, had no choice.

What a "Right to Birther" is doing is making certain that the "For Profit Prisons" have a new crop of inmates every year.

You call yourself "Right to Life" but what kind of life? Until you promise the basics for eighteen years, nutrition, love, education and opportunity, it is a misnomer to call it the, "gift of life." What it should be called is a "life sentence."

Once again, this is America not Christianica. A Democracy not a Theocracy.

While the Constitution certainly gives you the right to religious freedom, it doesn't give you the right to religious aggression.

Good   Christian   Man

If your beliefs are spiritual and righteous,
I will fight for your right to believe
what you believe.
If your beliefs are political, I will fight you.
Not physically. I wholeheartedly believed
Jesus when he said,
"Turn the other cheek."
Are you certain that your beliefs are the
only ones that should be
acknowledged and respected?
On more than one occasion,
something I was sure of,
was proven to be wrong.

Let's be clear.

Believing in bizarre stories written by
MEN and MEN ALONE who believed the
world was flat does not make you
a good person.
Being a good person
makes you a good person.
That reminds me of the mob hit man on
60 minutes who happened to be a Catholic.
He said that once he confessed to a
Catholic priest, the seventeen murders he
committed, he was forgiven by God
immediately, no if's and's or but's.

MONEY MONEY MONEY MONEY

While Americans weren't the first to monetize religion

—

see Vatican

We have certainly brought it to new heights

—

see Megachurch

The only church that I would belong to
is the church that refuses to take
a penny of my money.

That's faith in practice!

Patriotism?
"When stupidity is considered patriotism, it
is unsafe to be intelligent."

He Ain't Heavy

Most
humans
do better
when they believe they have help.

Believing in a higher power
helped
me
to
get
sober.

Religions were created
because
life becomes unbearable
at times.

The ~~Ten~~ 2 Commandments

The only real commandments necessary:

1. Honor thy mother and father unless **they're assholes or crackheads.**
2. Treat others the way you want to be treated.

It could've been a lighter load for Moses
'cause there's no need for the other eight.
Thou shalt not kill

—

see Capital Punishment

—

KC

It Can Be Confusing

If you're going to the library looking for the Bible,
would you look under fiction or nonfiction?
It depends on who your parents are.

‒

KC

Providing there are cell towers and a solar
charger, what would you rather have on a
deserted island:
Bible or iPhone?

‒

KC

Can you point to where in the Bible
it says
RACISM IS OKAY?
Because most of my religious friends
are racists.

‒

KC

"I certainly don't begrudge someone else their choice to follow whatever they do, it's just for me, it doesn't make sense. I think more harm has come to this planet through organized religion, probably, than any single situation that we've invented."

‒

Martin Mull

GOD
He's never to blame but always gets the credit.

Religions

Whenever and wherever humans believe in an
invisible dictator
that watches every move you make and
monitors every thought you have
there will be chaos.

Finally

If religion were the answer,
we'd have the answer.

With all these religions,
you'd think the world
would be in a better place.

Wars are started because of religion.
People are jailed and tortured
because of religion.
Hunger hasn't stopped because of religion.
Greed hasn't been conquered by religion.
Any and all of the good things
that religions do
could be done by a secular government run
by decent human beings.

Amen

Now the Political Part

d rump's knee is on America's neck.
The Republican Party **are** the three cops
that stood around and did nothing.

d rump has been a reminder of how easily

people can be controlled

and led to almost anywhere.

Pay attention.

Educate your children.

*I wonder why it is that a lot of the
same people who disregard the
warning on cigarette packs
also support
d rump?*

Sign in d rump's office:

The BUCKS stop here!

Why d rump puts his hands out
when he speaks:
The words
Amazing,
Greatest,
Longest
and Biggest
are written on the back of his fingers.
They're his cue cards.
One thumb says "Fake,"
the other says "News."
Without those 2 little hands,
he couldn't communicate.

The Sphincter Widening Act
of 2020

Mitch McConnell's new bill:

"The Sphincter Widening
Act
of 2020"

My bill will expand the
President's sphincter.
We've known for a long time that
the hole needed to be bigger.
My bill will allow five Senators
up the President's ass at one time,
seven if they're Rand Paul's size.

FOX BLUES

Are you news or entertainment?
I'd love to be at your arraignment.

It took awhile
but we found out
what your kind are all about.

You lie for cash
and stir it up
but finally your time is up.

We changed the channel long ago.
The sponsors left
I think you know.

I think for sure
they'll lock you up
and forever you'll shut up.

You made some money
that's for sure but
we finally found the cure.

Are you news or entertainment?
I can't wait for your arraignment.

When exactly did conservative become Stupid and Arrogant?

(see Martha McSally)

Notice I didn't call her Senator. She wasn't elected. Here's a Harvard educated woman with a solid reputation set to make a $60,000 a year pension from the Air Force, who **SOLD HER SOUL** after she lost her bid for the Senate and accepted an appointment by a Republican Governor for a $175,000
a year Republican hack job.
And she dared to call that CNN reporter a "Liberal Hack."
She wouldn't even wear a mask
until she was shamed into it.
She is such a terrible liar.
I would love to play poker with her.
This is your new Republican Party.

Thankfully, she lost to Mark Kelly making her a

TWO TIME LOSER.

Just because you have a degree,
doesn't mean you're smart.
(see d rump and Tucker Carlson)

Sometimes **EVIL** is misconstrued as smart

but it's **EVIL.**

To all the NBA players who won't criticize China:
"The slave owners would love you guys."

—

Pablo Torre, ESPN

You know your country has fallen behind when you argue about and need instructions to wear a face mask.

K̄C

Let me be clear to all the religious folks offended by my conclusions and opinions.
I've kept my mouth shut about your beliefs for over fifty years.

You opened a can of worms when *You* gave us d rump.

I wonder if in the future, you will still feel that the abortion judges were worth it?

"He'd be turning over in it
if he hadn't risen from it"

–
KC

Letters to Some Religious Friends:

This is the first letter I wrote to a friend of mine, a devout Catholic, after he said, "We should kill all the Muslims. Kill them all," he said. "The women and children, too?", I asked. He said, "All of 'em Kenny." He goes to church every Sunday.

Dear JV,   *written during the Iraq war*
You cannot just kill people and expect what caused them to become radical to just go away. Although I share your anger and sadness with the situation we find ourselves in as a country, I will never accept or condone total annihilation of a group of people as an answer.
First of all, it is an impossible task; secondly, it is morally inexcusable to slaughter innocent men, women and children in the name of righteousness.

Non-violent solutions are the ONLY long term solutions. The cold war and the civil rights movement proved that. Fighting in self defense is one thing. Invading another country with a culture totally different than ours based on shaky information and outright lies, is another.

All human beings are capable of atrocities when put in certain situations. In Vietnam, some of our soldiers committed atrocities while under duress. The picture of the Vietnamese boy being shot in the head at point blank, for being a suspected Viet Cong, that was on the cover of Time magazine, comes to mind. There are many other examples. No, they didn't slice his head off, they blew it off. You made a valid point about comparing the beheading of a human being to the abuse our soldiers committed in regards to the POWs in Iraq. But as our failure in Southeast Asia should have taught us, you cannot win these types of wars. The abuse committed by our soldiers will only serve to make a bad situation worse.

Do we want a solution or revenge? Solutions take time; revenge is too easy and solves nothing. As far as I know, no Iraqis were on any of the planes responsible for 9/11. Our country must always take the moral high road because if we don't, I fear that no one else will.

Our enemy was and is Al Qaeda. It should never become the Muslim faith. Why profess to believe in a loving, caring God, why make the sign of the cross or go to church if you ignore the teachings of Jesus himself? You cannot just kill people and expect what caused them to become radical to go away.   KC

Dear Jim,   *March 13, 2019*

Continuing our phone conversation....
Conservatives are taught to be afraid of everything.

Fear God
Fear change
Fear liberals
Fear brown people
Fear black people
Fear socialists
Fear, fear, fear!
Fear homosexuals. Fear different.
Fear the unknown. Fear, fear, fear!

If a person is afraid, they are easier to control.
Control is the goal. Donald Trump uses fear like a
master. Church leaders and that goes for any
church, want you to live life the way THEY see it.
They interpret the bible so that it fits into the way
THEY think life should be lived but that doesn't
necessarily mean it's right for everyone.
"Pro Life" should be "Pro Health Care" for all. I
find it hypocritical to lobby for the fetus only to let
a two year old die because the parents are too poor
to afford health care. If you were taught from the
same bible as I was, it should be clear that the
theme of Jesus Christ's teachings was Socialism.
Donald Trump is the most destructive, disgusting
human being who has ever been in the White
House. He and his family are grifters. They do not
care about others, especially others who can't
afford membership to Mara Lago or any of their
other tacky country clubs. Do you think Jesus
Christ would want to be a member of one of
Trump's private clubs? I think not.

I've had it with the hypocrisy of white evangelicals who hide behind the label of "Christian" in order to promote their earthly endeavors. A person either practices the teachings of Jesus Christ or they don't. Just claiming to be a Christian isn't enough. Prove it by actually practicing his teachings (Matthew 25:40-45).

Jim, what pissed me off so much was the name calling. You said that, "Democrats were murdering babies." You've been watching too much Fox TV. If destroying every institution that I grew up respecting is winning, I'd rather lose than win with Donald Trump.

Whatever happened to the "compassionate conservatives?" Was that just a political catch phrase? The breaking news isn't usually the whole truth and depending on what channel you're watching, it's getting harder and harder to know what's fact and what isn't. It really takes listening to both sides.

Happy to point out my truth,
Ken Champagne

When exactly did conservative
become a code word for racist?
Because most, if not all,
of my so-called
conservative acquaintances are racist.

$\bar{KC}$

Dear Jim,   *Sometime in 2020*

Although it contains everything necessary to become a tree, an acorn is not a tree and Democrats are not murdering babies in America. If your religious beliefs make you think that you should be able to tell a young girl in NY who's been made pregnant what she has to do with the rest of her life, then we will disagree forever. To me a fetus is not a baby. A baby is a baby. And so we disagree on that. That's why America was created so we could disagree and not hate each other or even worse.

While I'm not a member of any religion or political party, I was offended by your comment that Democrats were murdering babies. That's why I had to write. When you abort a fetus, you abort a fetus. When you murder a baby, you go to jail. But an acorn is not a tree. Not to me anyway.

Thank goodness this is America and not Christianica. Anti- abortion people would like to force a new crop of pissed off, hurt, uneducated, uncared for, future "for profit prison" inmates. But they don't want to pay to educate, feed, provide health care, love, you know, all the things human beings need to become productive.

So you're not just well meaning Christians wanting to save the lives of innocent helpless children. Actually, it's just the opposite. If you care about helping children there are plenty of them in cages down at the border. Help them! Remember you helped elect the guy who put them there.

Gladly pointing out my truth,
Ken Champagne

At the end of the introduction to this book I promised you the true meaning of success. Well, here it is:

SUCCESS

IS

QUIETING

THE VOICES

(I WROTE ABOUT ON PAGE 112)

Constitutional changes I see coming in the future of the United States

1. Vote to abolish the Electoral College.
2. You can own one rifle and one hand gun, no automatic weapons. Collectors can register to keep more but only 6 bullets per "collectors item."
3. Public health will be deemed more important than freedom of religion. You can worship but you can't contaminate non-believers.
4. Healthcare shall be deemed a constitutional right.
5. The President is not above the law and can be prosecuted. In addition, all presidential candidates must turn over 25 years of tax returns immediately upon filing to run.
6. All drugs will be made legal. The war on drugs will end and the treatment of drug addiction will begin in earnest.
7. All education will be free. In fact, the government will actually pay people to enter certain fields of study.

Sadly, I do not believe any of these changes to the Constitution will take place during my lifetime but I am convinced that they will one day be a part of the **"Constitution of the New United States of America."** A place where all human beings are considered equal under the law.

Book III

Shell Fragments

"There's a reason Aliens never land."

—

Mike Ryan, Executive Producer
Dan Le Batard Show with Stugotz

*I went through life like a swimmer
who is desperately trying to find the
shallow end of the pool.
Panicked, bouncing continually,
trying to keep my head above water.*

—

KC

Personal Power

I think I was in my 20's before I realized
that I had the ability to make someone
HATE ME
or
LAUGH SO HARD
they couldn't catch their breath

Drive Carefully

Don't try to figure out life.
Just enjoy the high moments
and go slow over the speed bumps.
If you hit a brick wall,
take care of the survivors,
bury the dead,
mourn and move on.

Talk About
Upside Down World
2020

We now have multiple cases of
WHITE people (cops) breaking
into **BLACK** peoples houses.
That's right.
Sometimes they're even
KILLING THEM.
And the only thing that the
black people
did wrong, was to be home at the
time of the break-in.

Zip Code Racist

My **father** was a **Zip Code Racist**
But not one of the real *EVIL* kind
He didn't have a hood in the closet
But he said **RACIST** things all the time

Like most people in a certain **Zip Code**
He just wanted to fit in at church
Or in his case the local bar
It was a small town
so there was nothing worse

He even had one **BLACK** friend
That he would drink with
from time to time
He brought him over to meet the kids
To make everything look fine

But my **father** was a **Zip Code Racist**
His cronies knew this to be true
Like Mr Leo across the street
If you were white he'd do anything for you

Not Bob Dylan

Would you even know Bob Dylan
If you passed him on the street?
And if you sat next to John Prine
Would you think to yourself
"How Sweet?"
And if John Lennon started talking
Would you recognize his voice?
And if someone asked who you liked best
Could you even make a choice?

There are unknown voices everywhere,
writing songs and telling tales.
I stop sometimes and listen to them,
when everything else I try fails.

The poets only tell us what's true.
You see, it's what they're here to do.
And what a feeling that'll come over you,
the day you discover that you're one, too.

This is a story about a friend worth having.
*Be kind to yourself. That friend is **you.***

Some

*Some people like **you***
some people don't
*some people **you** meet*
shove life down your throat
*but **you** don't have to eat it*
don't swallow
don't even chew
just keep repeating

*your life is up to **you***

Life IS an Occasional Suppository

It's not the big deal that we make it
it's really just an
endless surprise

though sometimes you feel you can't
take it
when you find out
the "truth" was all lies

but don't make a big deal about
nothing
it's just a big deal if you make it
'cause it's really just a typical story

Life IS an Occasional Suppository

Ink me baby!

Human beings are products of their generation.
There are some exceptions but they are rare.
This is why I grew my hair long and
kids today get

tattoos

I saw someone who I thought was "cool" and
mimicked them. Cuz we all want to be "cool."
But "cool" is generational. So what was "cool"
now isn't "cool" later.
**The real goal shouldn't be
to be "cool"
but rather comfortable with oneself.**
If a tattoo does that for you, then get a tattoo but
remember, it's with you forever.
Hair is not. Clothes are not. Styles change.
Because I am not of the tattoo generation,
I decided that my books would be my tattoos,
literary tattoos,
that will live on after I'm gone.

Tattoos

Dreams

I think I'll paint
with words tonight
It's the only way I can

I'll try to paint a picture
of dreams maybe I've had
or feelings I can't express
in any other way

If I don't paint
with words tonight
m y   d r e a m s
m a y   f a d e   a w a y

Time

There are so many things
that I'll never understand
like the sun and the sea
or the wind and the sand

Or barometric pressure
now where does that come from?
Or why some people seem
smart while others are
dumb?

But tonight, it's okay
no I don't have to know
why sometimes it's **fast**
and sometimes it's **slow**

Time

UnBrother

I was so glad you stood by me
when thick changed to thin
I was so grateful
I'm not really sure where to begin
We called each other "brother"
from the first time we met
but it seems that the word "brother"
hadn't been tested yet
I had a weak moment
maybe even two
and I often wondered
exactly what you'd do
So sorry your choice
was not what I'd hoped
the gossip and mean girls
with their usual tropes
you did what you had to
being just who you are
so, we're not really "brothers"

Unbrothers we are

IRIS

GOT THE CORONAVIRUS
FROM A GIRL NAMED IRIS

I MET HER ON SPRING BREAK
WHAT A BIG MISTAKE

WE WERE TOLD TO KEEP OUR DISTANCE
BUT WERE MET WITH NO RESISTANCE

WE WERE HOT AND WE KNEW IT
BUT THE FEVER REALLY BLEW IT

HOW COULD FEELINGS SO STRONG
TURN OUT SO WRONG

GOT THE CORONAVIRUS
FROM A GIRL NAMED IRIS

NEVER SAW HER AGAIN
SPRING BREAK'S OVER

THE END

AFFLUENT ACTING

They don't own the house
and they didn't buy the car
They're affluent acting
and it's working so far

But like all charades
It came to an end
They ran out of money
And had nary a friend

They don't own the home
broke the terms on the lease
Now the bill collectors
won't leave them in peace

Another repeat
same story retold
Another soul exchanged
for an empty bucket of coal

It seemed to stop working
it happened so fast
This phony charade
never meant to last

AFFLUENT ACTING

Upside down "ME TOO"

HE said NO!
SHE said YES!
Who would win?
It was anybody's guess?
I know the kind you talkin 'bout.
The kinda girl put her tongue in your mouth.
She could be from anywhere,
it's really hard to say.
But one thing that's for certain,
she's gonna get her way.
HE said NO!
SHE said YES!
Who would win?
It was anybody's guess?
Though it didn't happen often,
it happened more than once.
She thought he was attractive
and wanted him a bunch.
One day he said he'd had enough.
He'd grown tired of this abusive stuff.
But when he tried to push her away,
she said she'd have a lot to say.
I'll lie if I have to.
I'll tell 'em it was you.
And in this "ME TOO" atmosphere,
There'll be nothing you can do.
HE said NO!
SHE said YES!

FINE PRINT DISCLAIMER

This next piece is about the bad ice cream packaging that made me almost swallow a piece of plastic that was the same dark brown color as the fudge in the ice cream I was eating. This caused me to communicate with the first line of defense at Kroger Corporate.

Ya' ever notice how you can't get to anyone who matters any more. They've all hired deflectors. I believe it's an actual job title.

I responded to their response with my own **"Fine Print Disclaimer."**

Fine Print Disclaimer: These words should not be misconstrued as any type of a threat. We are just two old folks exercising their right to free speech. This letter, however, does contain a high dose of truth. The truth, when absorbed in large doses can cause discomfort. Remember, none of these letters would have been necessary had I been allowed to speak to the person who made the decision to use the packaging on your "high tier" ice cream. These letters are also not a precursor to any type of lawsuit or meant to harm anyone at Kroger in any way, shape, or form. SO, RELAX and think of all the time and money wasted because of "policy."

The Illusion

Freedom means so much to me.
Yes, we are **free** to make the rich richer.
Free to **work** for the rich.
Free to make rich people, richer still.
ARE RICH PEOPLE ESSENTIAL?
I want to tell you what "rich" means to me.
First, you get the best of everything on Earth.
Then, you get two times the best
of everything on Earth.
Once you have three times more than anyone else
of the best of everything on Earth,
that's enough.
I don't think rich is someone
with kids and a mortgage,
even if they make a lot of money.
But after you've acquired three times the best
of everything on Earth,
you are actually hurting yourself and those you
love because
you are not essential
and you are stealing money the
ESSENTIALS
deserve and will eventually demand.

Those Loopholes

This NPR program brought to you by:
A Rich Motherfucker and
The Rich Motherfucker's Wife Foundation.
How they got the money?
Your guess is as good as mine.
If they would've just paid their fair share of
taxes while they were alive, we probably
wouldn't even know their name,
nor would we need to.

Just the Facts Ma'am

One of the things that I have learned
about the "facts," is that most people don't
really want to know them. If the truth
doesn't fit into a belief that makes one feel
good, then it mustn't be the truth. Most
people do not want to believe that it all
ends at death so it is quite simple to get
them to follow a "truth" that says
otherwise.

Alienation Experts Inc.

FUCK YOU!

Specializing in Rude, Crude,
Abrasive and Abusive comments
Why ruin your reputation
Bad taste is our middle name
Put them in their place without leaving
your space
We make the annoying calls
We obtain the embarrassing photos
Unlimited Fuck You's
We do it all
We supply the rude, lewd, crude
and they'll never figure it out cuz we
never open our mouth

PhD in Dickology

Call: HEY-FU2-FUFU

Brains

Everybody's got to deal
with what they've got
You can't be something
that you're not
If you've got muscles
instead of brains
not even smart enough
to get out of the rain
you might have something
that I have not
But I've got something
that you haven't got
I've got brains
You know muscles aren't as
important
as they used to be
Nowadays you really have to
out think me
I've got brains
And I'll use them too
Best be careful
or I'll use them on you
I've got Brains

The Resting Inventors' Resort

Here's a thought that passed through my head.
What if the inventors had been lazy instead?
Just laying around like they had nothing to do.
Instead of inventing stuff for me and for you.
Picture a swimming pool,
thoughts flying all around.
But no one's taking notes, nothing's written down.
Who's that over there?
Maybe **Einstein** or **Bell?**
I think I just saw **Edison,**
maybe **Isaac Newton** as well.
The vibes were sure heavy.
Big thoughts were everywhere.
But when I looked closer,
not one of them seemed to care.
They weren't wearing their inventor clothes,
so I only recognized a few
But boy, did I become enlightened,
before the day was through
Computers are coming,
I heard one of them say.
We'll be flying in cars,
it'll happen one day.
They all seemed so friendly.
Famous figures everywhere.
But none of them seemed busy,
not one of them seemed to care.
'Cause this is the resting inventors' resort.
And here you're just another guy.
'Cause even though you're a famous inventor,
if you don't get some rest, you'll die.

Here's something I noticed lately:

Should **button** be pronounced
but in or **bud din?**
Should **Putin** be pronounced
Poot in or **Pood din?**
Should **kitten** be pronounced
kit in or **kid din**?

I've recently heard a White House reporter, a
Harvard educated sports personality and a
famous entertainer use these pronunciations.
What up with this, ya'll?
I'm thinking this new pronunciation is
generational since they all seem to be around
the same age.
Moreover,
no one I know says bud din,
Pood din or kid den. What surprises me is that
none of their peers have mentioned this to them.
Also, no one I know says
moreover.

Some Farts

Some farts	like to party down
Some farts	don't make a sound
Some farts	are down and dirty
Some farts	come out squirty
Some farts	will water your eyes
Some farts	will leave a surprise
Some farts	will stay, stay, stay
Some farts	will chase you away
Some farts	are really sad
Some farts	make people mad
Some farts	show no class
Some farts	just jump out your ass
Some farts	rumble and shake
Some farts	can be a big mistake
Some farts	are the Guliani type
	but you better check
	you might have to wipe
Some farts	make no bang or boom
	but those are the kind
	that can clear a room

Some Farts

244

POLITICIAN

Have you learned how to talk and say nothing
Have you learned how to lie with a straight face
They're two talents you'll be needin'
if you plan to succeed 'round this place
POLITICIAN
We see that you don't embarrass
when we catch you in a lie
Your face don't change expression
and it's got us wondering why
POLITICIAN
We know you have two mouths
even though we can't SEE them both
How do you keep a straight face
When you raise your hand to take the oath
POLITICIAN
Now they say there's a new generation
coming on the scene
Yes, a brand-new delegation
gonna get this city clean
POLITICIAN
When we figured out you lied
lied directly to our face
You made it very easy
to kick you out of this place

POLITICIAN

Please Don't Turn Away

can't watch this story
'cause I get too sad
when I heard what happened (again)
it made me fighting mad

looks like another horrific
tale about hate
seems they caught the assailant
but a little too late
they say he was a religious fanatic
what religion I'm not sure
so sad I've seen this behavior
too many times before

some tried to ask questions
'bout where he got the gun
now is not the time they said
there'll be time when this is done

can't watch this story
'cause I get too sad
when I heard what had happened (again)
it made me fighting mad

Naked and UnAfraid

I'm gonna stand here **in my underwear**
and scream at the top of my lungs
I'm gonna stand here **in my underwear**
until something finally gets done

I may even drop these draws
it's really up to you
I'm gonna stand here **in my underwear**
seems there's nothing left to do

maybe when you see me **naked**
crying, shaking in the crowd
seems you only pay attention
when it gets **ugly** and real **loud**

I'm gonna stand here **in my underwear**

Fragments

*You know, each **fragment** tells a story*
of exactly what happened here.
Pick up all the pieces
when the dust has finally cleared.

When you put them all together,
you know, the picture starts to clear.
*Turns out the **truth** is very **painful***
and exactly what we feared.

*You know, each **fragment** tells a story.*
Leave one out, it changes all.
Leave the color out of Springtime,
it could be mistaken for the Fall.

*The **fragments** will not lie to you.*
It's just something they cannot do.
*Put the **fragments** back together*
'cause it's the only thing to do.

Social Drinkers

Social drinking,
Why?
I've never actually known a
"social drinker."
You know, a person who drinks
"socially."
What the hell does that mean?
I think it means **happy, not sloppy.**

OOOHHHH, THAT L I N E...
You know, the one you should
never cross.
I was never able to see
THAT LINE
after I started drinking.
Oh, **I CROSSED IT**
but I never saw it when I did.

If a dog could live till thirty

You know the world wouldn't seem so dirty
If a dog could live till thirty
Chasing the ball and running all day long
Greeting me every day when I come home
Making sure I'm never ever alone

All the girls would be so flirty
If my dog could live till thirty
When your dog is cute
They act like you're cute too

And she always seems to have something
new to do

You know the world wouldn't seem so dirty
If a dog could live till thirty
Chasing the ball and running all day long
Greeting me every day when I come home
Making sure I'm never ever alone

Dedicated to Spirit The Dog
7/2006-8/21/2020

Well Meaning

My biggest complaint is that no one
prepared me for the real world. Like many
of us, I wasn't told the truth. I wasn't told
what life is really like. I didn't even know a
little. Painfully, I found this out very early in
my young adult years.

Prepare your children. If you shelter them
from the truth you are not preparing them,
you are setting them up.
Take 'em to a homeless shelter.
Take 'em to a jail.
If you don't teach 'em what life is really like,
you're setting them up to fail.
Tell the boys about the girls.
Tell the girls about the boys.
Tell 'em both about the liars
and all the other noise.
You should only tell your children the truth.
You can protect them for just so long.
You may think you are protecting them
but I promise you, you're wrong.
They probably won't live in the world you wish
for them. It's better they know the truth at a
young age, rather than getting
slapped in the face by it later in life.

Jesus, Table of Four

Jesus fed the multitudes.
He didn't just get enough
loaves and fishes
for a table of four.
I often marvel at people who
call themselves
Christian and Capitalists.

Jesus had no capitalist
tendencies, none!
You can twist it
to it your narrative.
But
Jesus was a Socialist!

Getting to Know You

While I did not agree with a military draft, I believe one year of **"Civic Service"** should be required at age 18. That service should be completed in a part of the country different from where you were raised. Participants should be used in a similar manner as the **CCC** was used in the **1930's,** upgrading the task to coincide with what is needed in today's society. **ALL citizens, male, female, transgender, rich, poor, ALL.** (Very limited hardship deferments). Bringing together: **all religions, all races, all sexual preferences. All Americans.** Most every problem in this country could be solved if we knew each other better.

The Marketers

My life was marketed to me
and yours was marketed to you

They told us what to eat and drink
They told us what to do

They even told us what to drive
Our lives were sold to us

We bought a little everyday
And never made a fuss

Now that I'm a little older
I give marketing a bad rap

'Cause when I look around me
I never needed all this crap

USA Taliban

If the South rises again, we're Fucked.
They have all the guns and trucks.
Remember when we saw Isis on TV,
driving all the white Toyota pick-ups?
I think it's possible that in this country,
we may have the Christian version of the
Taliban but with one difference.
They'll be driving around in
white Ford F150's

What's the difference between
A Christian Radical
A Jewish Radical and
A Muslim Radical?

Fashion

A Child of the Old South

Growing up in the Jim Crow south but
not being a racist myself,
it really touches my heart that there
are so many interracial couples in
commercials on TV these days. But the
marketers have gone overboard. So
much so, that I believe I saw
a brand new race of humans in a
car ad the other day.

Got Hypocrisy?

The nuns of my generation wore
uniforms they called "habits,"
which exposed only a small portion
of the woman's face.
These outfits weren't much different
than the hijabs worn by Muslim women.
But I don't remember hearing any
criticism of what the nuns wore.

"kennys dick"

One evening recently, my wife and I were kidding around about genitalia, when I said, "Let's see if there's anything on the internet about my dick." So, we typed in **"kennys dick."** Here's what we found.

The urban dictionary defines **"kennys dick"** as something that is too small to see and needs viagra to keep it up.

Although that wouldn't have been accurate in the seventies, it is most accurate today.

How do they know so much?

Reptile Love

I'm a lizard lad
And I love my life
I'm a lizard lad
and I'm lookin' for a wife

See this RED THING
pokin' out my chin
Come mere baby
it's time to begin

Now I'm a lizard lady
And I'LL tell YOU when
YOU better wait for my signal
before you begin

'Cause I like a little courtship
There'll be time for the dirty deed
Show me that RED THING again
and I'll give you what you need

Life Is Short

Since the beginning of time, **men** have always done whatever is necessary to have **sex**. The **women** of my generation liked **"cat calls"** and were offended if you didn't mention something about their body. **Talking dirty** was normal, **expected** and a **welcome** sign of attraction. Back then, it was about looks. That's just the way it was, whether you like it or not. Somewhere along the way, someone changed the rules. By the way, **women** have always been in charge anyway. Don't blame **men** because you finally figured that out. Don't blame us because of your mother or grandmother's **complicity**.

Now, put on a bra and button your blouse. And quit being so angry all the time.

A Penis Once Again

Males are born with
PENISES.
As they get older, these
PENISES
become
DICKS.
On occasion, these dicks become
COCKS,
which is the only time they're of real
value.
As we continue to age, the
COCKS
show up less and less
and the
DICKS
become
PENISES
once again.

My Kids

Writing books is actually better than having children. You can totally control what goes in them and how they look. They can make you happy, they can disappoint and just like children they actually get "sick" sometimes.
Some go out and become successful, while others fail miserably.

No Blame

There is definitely a percentage of humanity that is inherently stupid. It's not even their fault. I'm not certain but they may be related to the people in every society that don't give a shit. Even educating some people doesn't make them smarter.

Gang Colors and Symbols

Bloods......**Red**
Crips.........Blue
Republicans. ......Maga hat/
                         rebel flag
Jews.......**Star of David necklace**
Christians...... Crucifix **necklace**
Sikhs........turb**an**

Do your religious beliefs make you
compassionate or **arrogant?**
There are some that wear their
religious swag like
Gang Colors

"You can choose your friends
but you sho' can't choose your family"

—

Harper Lee

The Choice

How different a person's life would be
if a *fetus* could *choose*
its family.
Just where it would live
and go to school.
In fact, I think, that would be
way cool.
'Cause if we all came out
where we wanted to be,
how different a person's life would be.
If a *fetus* could *choose*
its family.

Money or Fun

If you do everything for money, when you die, people who didn't work for it will get the money that YOU earned. And YOU will be dead. If you do things for fun, when you die your life would've been fun. Would you rather have money or fun? While fun doesn't necessarily take money, money doesn't always translate into having fun.

It Takes All Kinds

One of the most difficult aspects of life for me to accept is that on more than one occasion, I've been surrounded by simple-minded, ignorant Motherfuckers. And since there was a time when I was a simple-minded, ignorant, Motherfucker, I know how they think and how they look. I wrote this to let you know you're not alone.

Every Twenty Years

Isn't it strange that the world we grow up in, is
rarely the world we live in as an adult? I found that
the world completely changes every twenty years.
1951–1971
Two completely different Americas.
2000–2020
Two completely different worlds.

Housekeeping

You can either be the guest at the hotel
or the one who cleans the room.
Two lives, two completely
different experiences.
Life is a gift for one
and a life sentence for the other.

Karen and Chad

She always seemed so angry
And she was easily made mad
She was raised to think she was special
A twinkle in the eye of her dad
Although their wedding was a big deal
And everyone seemed glad
No one could see what was to come
In the lives of Karen and Chad
Oh, they had the big house
In the right neighborhood
Just like Chad told Karen they would
But things are changing in Whiteville
The colors are changing you see
Interracial couples are moving in
And altering the scenery
Seems they were raised in a white world
A world that no longer exists
And it seems that Karen, yes Karen
Has started pitching hissy fits
She's called the police
To say "black men are near"
But she couldn't explain
What exactly she feared
Did they say something ugly?
Did they threaten her with knives?
Or were they just living
Black People Lives

Nowhere

Who built the highway to Nowhere?
And how did I end up there?
Must've been driving in the wrong
direction,
without even being aware.

There's not much to do in Nowhere,
not many interesting folk.
Me ending up in Nowhere,
must be some kind of practical joke.

Who built the highway to Nowhere?
And how did I end up there?
Must've been driving in the wrong
direction,
without even being aware.

Now, if you find yourself in Nowhere,
it's probably 'cause of you.
You were driving in the wrong direction
and ended up in Nowhere, too.

THE MAGIC

SOMETIMES I SIT AND WRITE NOTHING
EVEN THOUGH I'VE GOT SOMETHING TO SAY
I'M STILL NOT SURE WHY IT HAPPENS
WHY THE WORDS JUST WON'T COME MY WAY

BUT AS YOU CAN SEE I'M WRITING NOW
I'M WRITING, THAT'S PLAIN TO SEE
THE WORDS I NEEDED STARTED COMING
MY PEN STARTED WORKING WITH ME

YES, IT SEEMS THAT IT HAPPENED AGAIN
THE MAGICS RETURNED TO MY PEN
SEEMS I'VE SAT LONG ENOUGH TO THINK UP
SOME STUFF
SO I'M WRITING IT DOWN

THE END

Unaware

If you were sharing your life with

Vincent van Gogh,

would you even care?

Would you even know?

And would his artistic genius even show

if you were sharing your life with

Vincent van Gogh?

⚜⚜⚜⚜⚜⚜⚜⚜⚜⚜⚜⚜

"Swell" and "Much obliged"

When did they stop being used?

I'm pretty sure "*swell*" stopped being used

when men stopped wearing hats.

And *"much obliged"* left us

after Bonanza was canceled.

NATURE

Sadness for some is dinner for others.
If all of this was created by an
ALL POWERFUL, ALL LOVING GOD,
THEN WHY
does something have to die
for something else to live?
Where's the love in that?

The bigots, racists and religious fanatics
will go kicking and screaming
into the future.
But science, fact and actual knowledge will
overtake them like a tidal wave.
Truth will eventually rule.

Rachel Maddow wrote a book about
Spiro Agnew.
That's like writing a book about a kid who
liked Shemp more than Curly.
Do you know anyone
who got excited when
Shemp filled in for Curly?

⚜⚜⚜⚜⚜⚜⚜⚜⚜⚜⚜⚜

Everyone has
"a turd that wouldn't go down after flushing"
story. This got me to thinking, why is it that
we're so afraid to let someone else see our
poop? What's up with that?
Why is it so embarrassing?
It's terrifying to some. But why?

⚜⚜⚜⚜⚜⚜⚜⚜⚜⚜⚜⚜

Know someone well
before you confide in them.
This one is very important!
Even someone you consider a good friend is
capable of selling you down the river.

Closing Time
**I was nudging up against the "too late"
and I still didn't know what to do.
You know, running out of
"conversational gas"
and it was getting late.**

Testicles
If you don't have testicles,
you have no idea what it's like to have
them and the power they have.

If the educated class has a motive for
spreading certain propaganda,
it can be extremely time consuming
and difficult to find out what that motive is.

The Founding Fathers weren't so smart.
1) they owned other people and thought it was OK.
2) they thought everyone could handle a gun.
These are two major flaws, wouldn't you say?

There are so many people
who are more talented than me.
What will I do? The best I can.
Yes, it's that simple.

It's been my experience that
most people are brave in some way. Even wimps
can be brave on occasion. I have had personal
experiences that have surprised the hell out of me.
You'd be amazed what a person can do if they have
no other choice.

273

Mirror, Mirror on the Wall

Don't feel so bad, MOST of us are not attractive and even attractive people are only temporary

The shoe store salesman:
"It's boiled wool."
Ken: "I don't care if it's
boiled, baked or deep fried,
that's too much money for a slipper."

Nothing really changes
but fashion
and even fashion
comes around again
eventually

If prostitution were legal, maybe the
"Proud Boys"
wouldn't be so jacked up all the time.
Maybe they'd be the
"Relaxed Boys" or the "Laid Back Boys."

⚜⚜⚜⚜⚜⚜⚜⚜⚜⚜⚜⚜

Republican:
"I've got mine, Fuck you."
Trump Republican:
"I've got mine and yours,
Fuck you."

⚜⚜⚜⚜⚜⚜⚜⚜⚜⚜⚜⚜

The oldest man never dies,
neither does the oldest woman.
There's always a new one waiting in the wings
to immediately take their place.

I wonder every year around
Thanksgiving,
why people risk their lives to go to see
people they really can't stand.

Because of caring
too much about the fetus,
you are electing officials
who don't care about the living.

Anti–Masturbation Law

Would a man allow a woman to tell him what he
can and cannot do with his body?
What gives a man the right to waste sperm
that should be used to procreate?
After all, it's pre fetus sperm.

Praycare

Some parents use religion because they are either too busy, too lazy or incapable of teaching right from wrong themselves.

The truth is, like a lot of things, a woman's breasts were not that big of a deal until someone made seeing them off limits.

Shallow?

Tell me who goes out at night looking for the most unattractive person they can find?

Manizers

If I was a womanizer,
what were the women?

My education, though unorthodox to
some, has taught me that the truth is not
always easy to find but is
ALWAYS worth searching for.

"Religious freedom?"
What about Secular freedom?
You know, freedom to believe things based on
actual scientific fact?

I realized as I got older that there was yet another good reason not to have children, THEIR PARENTS.

TO THE "GOD CREATED EVERYTHING" PEOPLE;
DID GOD CREATE THE GOOD PEOPLE FIRST
OR THE SLEAZY ONES?

Life is not only about winning
but also losing by a nose.
Be prepared for both.

Before you claim that something in this book offends you, at least I didn't record W.A.P. Although I wish I would have.

Never take "No" for the final answer. "No" means maybe later but just not now. So take a step back and ask again later.

DON'T ASSUME THAT PEOPLE AUTOMATICALLY FEEL THE SAME WAY YOU DO. IN FACT, NEVER ASSUME ANYTHING.

**All colors accepted here.
Especially off colors.**

Before you have children,
ask yourselves this question:
What will they do for a living?

Too High, Too Hard
Not a baseball story
My life in the 70's

Most people don't really want to hear or be
shown the truth if it's ugly.
Sometimes the truth is awful.

It's hard sometimes to be kind to sick
people. Always remember,
it's harder to be sick.

❖❖❖❖❖❖❖❖❖❖❖❖❖

They don't seem to teach two very
important subjects anymore,
Sportsmanship and Civics.

❖❖❖❖❖❖❖❖❖❖❖❖❖

<u>WE</u> MAKE THINGS MATTER.
IF WE DIDN'T, NOTHING WOULD.

DON'T BE A FOLLOWER
YOU'LL ALWAYS HAVE YOUR NOSE UP
SOMEONE ELSE'S ASS

Shit to Roses
Isn't it ironic that manure is the reason
roses smell so good?

Don't blame the men from the last generation.
They learned from the previous generation.

You can dislike "a black person"
and not be a racist.
But if you dislike black people
You are a racist. So shut up.

⚜⚜⚜⚜⚜⚜⚜⚜⚜⚜⚜⚜⚜⚜

My readers tell me that they actually learned
more about themselves
than they did about me while reading
"The Shell Books."

⚜⚜⚜⚜⚜⚜⚜⚜⚜⚜⚜⚜⚜⚜

Make sure your children know the
difference between fact and opinion.
Even yours.
Especially yours.

WORKING HARD WON'T MAKE YOU RICH.

HOWEVER, IT MAY ENRICH YOU.

⚜⚜⚜⚜⚜⚜⚜⚜⚜⚜⚜⚜

Time + Inquiry + Intellect = Wisdom
All parts need be present to reach sum

⚜⚜⚜⚜⚜⚜⚜⚜⚜⚜⚜⚜

IF YOU LOSE YOUR TEMPER,

YOU USUALLY LOSE.

COMPOSURE DUMBFOUNDS OTHERS.

⚜⚜⚜⚜⚜⚜⚜⚜⚜⚜⚜⚜

Pay attention to red flags,
especially in matters of the heart.
You probably won't but I had to try.

Remember, if you plan on growing old,
you will need good
"Old People Karma."
So be nice.

AGAINST ABORTION?
ADOPT A CHILD AND
MIND YOUR OWN
BUSINESS!

No better feeling than a job you enjoy.
No worse feeling than a job you hate.

Be careful when you judge others harshly.
They might just be right.

Do breasts have gills?
No, that's why women have cleavage.

I believe insecurity is taught or conditioned.
Therefore, it can be untaught.

Homosexuality is as natural as heterosexuality.
If you look at Nature,
you'll see it all around you.

NOTHING IS FREE.

IT MAY BE INCLUDED BUT IT IS NOT FREE.

Save Me

FROM THE MARKETING

IT'S ALREADY GOT MY WIFE

Save Me

FROM THE MARKETING

THAT'S RUINING MY LIFE

Greatness
is not always blatant.
In fact, it is subtle
more times than not.

And now, some One Liners or
a little more
Edgy Mark Twain

⚜⚜⚜⚜⚜⚜⚜⚜⚜⚜⚜⚜

Fuck always gets a capital "F"

⚜⚜⚜⚜⚜⚜⚜⚜⚜⚜⚜⚜

A vagina **IS** a pre-existing condition.

⚜⚜⚜⚜⚜⚜⚜⚜⚜⚜⚜⚜

If I'm not the strangest person at the party,
I'm leaving.

⚜⚜⚜⚜⚜⚜⚜⚜⚜⚜⚜⚜

Do not trust people
that you don't trust.

Never argue with a cop or a clerk.

When shoveling manure, it is always better to think of the hot bubble bath that awaits you, whether it does or not.

Never let anyone wear their shoes in your house, especially male travelers from Las Vegas, NV.

The world turned out to be something
I really didn't care for but
the alternative was even less appealing

How many times do you have to look behind
the curtain before you know
the wizard is a fraud?

I was beside myself but
I only had a ticket for one.

The longer you stay in your slice of the
Universe,
you start believing that IT IS the Universe.

*The amount of **education** you get is
directly related to the amount of **ass** you'll
have to **kiss** later in life.*

The people I've enjoyed most in life
have been strangers.

COVID-19
I saw a woman signing for the deaf with
little tiny masks on all her fingers.

If you continually put yourself down,
you open the door for others to join you.

While planning is important, most real good things
happen by chance.

It takes an ignorant person
to put down the poor and ignorant.

⚜⚜⚜⚜⚜⚜⚜⚜⚜⚜⚜⚜

What do you call a fat Lobbyist?
A Slobbyist.

⚜⚜⚜⚜⚜⚜⚜⚜⚜⚜⚜⚜

If you hired a rapper for your
daughter's birthday, would he then be a
gift wrapper?

⚜⚜⚜⚜⚜⚜⚜⚜⚜⚜⚜⚜

If her pants were any lower,
she could pee without taking them off.

Many years ago, I stopped following
and started practicing.

Be quiet before speaking and ask a lot of
questions before signing anything.

Rejection is
"God's" way of protecting you...
whatever "God" is?

GET MARRIED AS LATE IN LIFE AS POSSIBLE
AND HOPEFULLY TO YOUR BEST FRIEND.

Try to pay cash for everything,
understanding
"wants" are different than "needs."

Integrity is the only human trait that doesn't age.

Never drink with your boss

or

at a company party.

Always back into your parking space just in
case you need to get out in a hurry.

Most every time I've followed the crowd,
I ended up in the wrong place.

I want to live in a world where people
only die of natural causes.

The people who say family is the most
important thing in life are usually broke.

Nobody is ever as happy
as somebody selling something.

❦❦❦❦❦❦❦❦❦❦❦❦❦

Always send a handwritten thank you,
get well or sympathy card via **US mail.**

❦❦❦❦❦❦❦❦❦❦❦❦❦

*You can expect my best because I
expect my best.*

❦❦❦❦❦❦❦❦❦❦❦❦❦

Charm and dependability
rarely come in the same package.

If you're not taught something,
should you be condemned for not knowing it?

Most people are trained,
a smaller percentage actually think.

When I'm uncomfortable, I become
less than what I am capable of.

Life pretty much repeats itself with
different clothes.

Anytime you censor the opinion of others,
you diminish the value
of your own opinion.

You can let the world change you

or you can change the world!

"Every thief thinks everyone else is a thief."

—

Dan Le Batard's mother, Lourdes
(God, I love these people!)

To all the mothers:
Would you want a mother like you?

One of the hardest things in life for me
is watching truly sleazy people get ahead.

You can beat up a kid pretty bad
without even touching them.

It stops being a statement of individualism
when everybody does it.

Before you get all full of yourself,

remember,

all human beings are temporary.

In the heart, on the tongue,
out of the mouth = Pure Honesty.

I believe an abortion is actually
a gift to an unwanted fetus.

The only way to find out if you're any good, is to
share what you do with those who are great at it.

How great it would've been to have
an older brother like Wally Cleaver.

Old age don't care
how much money you got.

The only person that is better than you,
is a person who doesn't die.

If the bible is such a Holy book,
why do white supremacists quote it so often?

ONCE YOU ADMIT AND ACCEPT WHO YOU ARE,

LITTLE CAN HURT YOU.

If life is such a gift, why do we all need
"a reason" to live?

If someone confronts me with a
pit bull or a gun, they win.

SADLY, MOST PEOPLE DON'T EVEN REALIZE
THERE IS A BOX TO THINK OUTSIDE OF.

Don't cheat, don't lie and you'll be
married till the day you die.

If you wouldn't do it in a crowd,

it's probably best you don't do it

It's so easy to be happy and benevolent
when you're rich.

You get more "Good Mornings" while riding a
bike than you'll ever get while riding in a car.

WHAT GOOD DOES IT DO TO CALL A
STUPID PERSON, STUPID?

I recently had my craw removed.

The big corporations are making out like teenagers.

It's not possible to know what's possible.

I don't want to live anywhere I need a shop vac.

Education is cheaper than Incarceration.

MARKETING NEVER SLEEPS.

❦❦❦❦❦❦❦❦❦❦❦❦❦

Everyone knows something you don't.

❦❦❦❦❦❦❦❦❦❦❦❦❦

Most people only matter for a while.

❦❦❦❦❦❦❦❦❦❦❦❦❦

Even the famous go unknown with time.

❦❦❦❦❦❦❦❦❦❦❦❦❦

The second look, make sure you take it.

The "Suits" are the reason life sucks.

⚜⚜⚜⚜⚜⚜⚜⚜⚜⚜⚜⚜

Progress is sure Fucking up Earth.

⚜⚜⚜⚜⚜⚜⚜⚜⚜⚜⚜⚜

There should be a weight limit on spandex.

⚜⚜⚜⚜⚜⚜⚜⚜⚜⚜⚜⚜

"I never knew the beauty of Costco."

—

Post Malone

⚜⚜⚜⚜⚜⚜⚜⚜⚜⚜⚜⚜

If I'm half crazy, the other half is asleep.

Be a sponge, not a hose.

Always be early, never late.

Give more than you get.

Ego is the most costly human trait.

Masturbation saves at least two lives.

A giver gets more than a taker
could ever steal.

Dogs should live to be 30 or older.

Even if you're sure, don't be sure.

The only way to be great, is to be great.

You are not lost if you have a full tank of gas.

The next generation doesn't care what we think.

Do the right thing and you can't go wrong.

Racism is learned.

If you're next to nothing are you alone?

Suicide is not painless.

I try to never have two conversations with a racist.

Never let your genitals make important decisions.

SPEAKING OF WOLF BLITZER...
IS THERE A FLOBEE FOR BEARDS?

The Earth IS flat in some spots.

We all fail at something.

Our Constitution is so outdated it has become dangerous.

Note: Maybe you've noticed that most of the one and two liners ended up together at the end of some of the books.

It was tough but I explained to all the paragraphs, that once you grow to a certain size, you can no longer hang with the one liners.

You are automatically moved up to a place in the book equal in status to the amount of effort it took to create you. In the end, they bought into it.

End of Note.

Final Thought

I'm neither ashamed nor proud of my
LIFE.
Some parts I could've done without.
Certainly, I would've done many
things differently with proper
instruction, training and
LOVE.
My life was something that
happened while in close proximity to
ME.

Book IV

Shell Dust

Seventy Years

Bearded Kenny

You know Ken,
it would be helpful if you weren't you.

Special Dedication to this Chapter

To everyone,
(and there were quite a few of you),
who said that I wouldn't live to see
the age of 25,

hahahahahahahahahaha

I might not be dancin' but I'm still here.

Rejoice!
There is something to alienate almost everyone
in "The Shell Books."

Irony

Battling through bouts of depression,
sciatica, and loneliness, I didn't quit. For
some reason, my wimpy little ass kept
getting up, kept moving on, kept showing
up. Not bad for a crybaby, sissy, punk, bitch.
Ironically, most of my critics are dead.

Relax

I don't write for Malcolm Gladwell's audience.
I write for the people who clean his house and
cut his lawn. So please, relax and enjoy.

Anderson Cooper's Pretzel Logic

The next time you see Anderson Cooper conduct
an interview, watch how he ties himself in a
knot like a pretzel when asking a question.
I mean ya know, it's sorta
I mean ya know,
I mean ya know, ...

Scott Pelly's Prayer
(on bended knee)

To the god of all anchors
I pray to you Walter Kronkite
Please help me to not sound so pompous

There are at least fifty thousand great musicians
in the world. Why is it that only about five
make a good living?

Hey Kenny

Hey Kenny, what do you believe in?

1. Working to pay my way

2. Eating and Pooping

3. Saying I'm not sure when I'm not sure

4. Telling children the truth, as early as possible

5. Pulling for the underdog

I also hope reincarnation is a real thing and that there is a "fetus line" that you are put back into after you die. My hope is that by then they'll give you a choice. My choice is to come back as an inanimate object. I'd like to come back as a picture frame at the Louvre so that I could be surrounded by the world's most incredible art. And I wouldn't even be expected to comment.

So this is what it's *really* like?

At the age of 4 or 5, I witnessed my Cocker Spaniel being put into a car to be taken to the country "for her own good." I'm 70 and I've never forgotten that. You should never take a little boy's puppy, especially without talking to him first. It was devastating.

At nine or ten I was sexually molested by an older boy in scouting.

For the seventeen years I lived in my father's house, I can't remember him saying anything nice to me. I am certain that "I love you, son" was not in his vocabulary.

During my first year at St John Prep, a seminary for young men who think they have a "calling," Danny Kramer, the smartest, kindest, nicest boy lost his leg to cancer. The next year he lost his life. All the studying and hard work he did for nothing. Why study and work hard just to die at fourteen? I was now starting to have a very different outlook on life. It felt scarier and unpredictable. Danny

Kramer's death and the evening news of the 1960's changed my outlook on life forever. I became cynical that sophomore year of high school and that cynicism has never gone away. I have not seen life as a gift since. I can't even imagine what COVID-19 and the rump years have done to the kids of this generation.

In the mid 1960's they started shipping bodies back home from Vietnam. The gift of life was starting to feel less and less like a gift.

Around this same time, I was discovering that I had been lied to about girls. They weren't all sugar and spice and everything nice. And just like the boys, they were capable of lying too.

Next came my twenties. I buried so many friends during the next ten years, if I would've owned stock in a funeral parlor, I'd be wealthy.
Cynical?

And look, I realize others have had much worse childhoods than mine but our lives are personal aren't they. So too our pain.

My Life Today

The first part of my life wasn't anything like it is now. I'm sitting in a recliner, the sun is rising, coloring the sky in reds and golds and at this moment,
I'm glad I didn't quit.

Suicide

I write about my being afraid of
everything, in order to show folks
who are afraid of everything,
that doing well is possible.
Although I'm not the first to say life is
hard, I'm glad I didn't quit. And there were
times it could've gone either way.
What I'm trying to say is,

Don't Kill Yourself

Enough is Enough

As soon as you realize that you have enough money to live for the rest of your life, you should stop working for money.

Unless Judy Woodruff, Wolf Blitzer and Andrea Mitchell are working for free, they should be ashamed. Let the younger generation have a chance to make a living. Plus, it's sad to watch you all slow down, start to stutter and stammer.

With life expectancy rising, it's just not fair to stay in jobs past your prime. Especially, when a whole new crop of journalists are trying to support their families.

Lost Trust

During the early part of my life,
I completely respected and
totally trusted:

1. Priests
2. Doctors
3. Police
4. The News
5. Adults in general
6. Hitchhikers- yes, hitchhikers
    Now, I'm not so sure

Phony Sincerity

*"The key to success is sincerity,
if you can fake that,
you've got it made."*

George Burns

Gift of Life

As soon as I realized that we were all required to return this "gift," I stopped seeing life as a "gift" and instead started looking at life as an exercise. Sometimes I feel like exercising, sometimes I don't.

Luck

You know, I've never understood luck.
Why it's good or why it's bad.

But what I do understand is that you should be ready for it when it happens.

Luck

The Suits

are the problem

As soon as a man puts on a suit and gets a title,

he changes.

He thinks he's smarter.

He becomes more demanding,

more of a weasel,

less compassionate.

I think it's by design.

Look, it even happened to me.

I no longer even own a necktie.

Money makin Kenny

Saturday Night Fever

I've eaten with the **hoi**

had drinks with the **polloi**

And when I was young

there weren't many
pleasures

I didn't enjoy

But as I grew older

It just didn't seem right

To be hangin with the
"Haves"

Every Saturday night

Equality

I've always felt that prostitution
should've been legalized
at the same time as abortion.
I strongly believe in an individual's right
to choose their own destiny.

Parenting

As soon as you can tell them there is no
Santa Claus, as soon as you can tell them
life is hard, as soon as you can expose
them to reality, as soon as you can, tell
them the truth. Your job is to prepare,
not pamper.

Tell them the truth.

More on Parenting

If you frighten your children to death, they will not be able to handle any confrontation as adults. They will also probably be afraid of public speaking. And I think you should know, you can frighten them in more ways than you think. Yelling or talking too loud (threatening) are the obvious ways. But passive aggression can be just as frightening. And as an added bonus your children are acquiring these traits directly from you through osmosis, continuing the cycle.

Even More on Parenting

You should never make a child
eat anything.
I was once made to sit at the supper
table from 5 pm until my father went to
bed around 10 pm. I have never
forgotten that feeling. The food I
refused to eat was canned asparagus.
I gagged every time
it got close to my mouth.
What a stupid thing to do to a child.
And what an asshole my father was.

*Note: Now it's true that I've never
been a parent but I have been a child.*

Father's Day

Here's an idea dad,
why not teach your boys how to
diffuse a fight before you teach them
HOW to fight.

Guns

Well, you know, he's a hunter.
Why?
Doesn't he know you can buy food
or
does he just enjoy the killing?

Big Game Hunters

These guys chase a frightened,
unarmed creature until it's exhausted,
then shoot it dead. Now, as if they
accomplished something heroic, they
have someone take their picture with
the dead creature. And most religious
people support this behavior.

Big Game Hunters

Worker bee

I was raised to be a "worker bee"
educated just enough
to make a salary
get a job
make a some a doe (Italian)
that was all you needed to know
it matters not
if you like it or not
you should be happy
with the money you got
I was raised to be a "worker bee"

Should an education just be for
income purposes? I don't think so.
An education should help your life
experiences become larger and it
should be an equal opportunity for
every American.

A Comment from Roberta

I hired a masseuse to give Ken leg massages for his conditions. She came over 3 or 4 times and then she quit. She said, "Your husband is boning, groaning and farting during the massages." I said, "Why do you think I hired you?"

Not in a Million Years

I envision that one day my work, these books, the 5 books of "A Boomer Bible" will be handled by archaeologists and scholars wearing white gloves in a climate controlled room.
Hey, none of us will ever know!

Ah, The Family

My wife and I didn't have any children. We were both drunks and knew it would probably not be a good idea to procreate. Lately, I've heard a lot of people complaining about how hard it's been to be with their children so much.

What the Fuck did you think having children was all about? Plus, children are usually a reflection of their parents. Maybe you're the assholes.

A Comment on Poverty

There are two price points for an object. You can only afford the lowest price point. The object breaks within three months and you have to replace it. The people who could afford the higher price point bought a product that will last for years and comes with a warranty.
Get It?

Choices

When choosing your TV
entertainment:

"You needa the coda book"
from Marx Brothers-"A Day at the Races"

*direct tv, xfinity, cox cable, dish, xfinity
plus, disney plus, hulu, netflix, hbo,
hbo max, starz, you tube, philo, at&t
tv +, espn+, facebook watch, twitch,
sling, roku, apple tv +, peacock,
peacock premium,
fubo tv, amazon prime,
paramount +....*

So this is what civilization has come to?

The Future

*I've been waiting for the future
my whole life.
If you were in your future,
would you recognize it?
I'm actually living the future
that I imagined for myself in
the 1980's.
What will your future look like?*

Not Typical

*When I was a boy, my father
wanted me to grow up and be*

A MAN

but when I looked around at

the **MEN** *I saw,*
*I realized that not only didn't I want
to be like them, but more than
likely,
I could never be a typical*

MAN

Most of my life
I've been compelled to talk
about things I don't really
care about
in order to fit in.

Cheating

Athletes cheat

Taxpayers cheat

Husbands cheat

Wives cheat

Students cheat

Businesses cheat

Politicians cheat

Cheaters cheat

Oh Yeah, Horse Trainers
cheat!

The Important Stuff at 20

If asked for the list of the top ten most important things in my life from the ages of 20 to 30, this would be the list:

1. Sex

2. Sex

3. Sex

4. Sex

5. Sex

6. Sex

7. Sex

8. Job

9. Music, Alcohol and Drugs
   (Yes, they all go together)

10. Food- Ya gotta eat!

The Important Stuff at 70

1. *Wake up*-if this doesn't occur, disregard the following 9

2. *Pee*

3. *Sit in recliner*

4. *Stare*

5. *Drink coffee/eat THC granola*

6. *Read internet*- Yahoo, CNN breaking news, Bing and NOLA.com to see who died

7. *Work on books*

8. *Eat another THC edible*

9. *Pee*

10. *Go back to Bed*

*You know you're getting old when the sports stars you looked up to have **sons** who are already in **coaching.***

The Bearded Man and the Mirror

There's an old face under there.

An old face I'm not sure I want to see.

There's an old face under there,

that has become me.

Yeah, I think about shavin',

think about it every day.

But there's an old face under there

that keeps getting in the way.

There's an old face under there.

I think I'll let it be.

There's an old face under there.

A face I'm not sure I want to see.

Old Skin

Lets see now,
where to begin?
I'm not even certain,
just exactly where it's been.

It's been with me my whole life.
It helped me win my wife.
It's been red and it's been pink.
I've even seen it brown, I think.

It helps to keep my blood in.
It's been with me since the
beginnin'.
But you know sometimes
it's been a bitch.
It's acted up
and started to itch.

Sometimes it's been thin.
Sometimes it's been thick.
But tonight it seems old
and it happened pretty quick.

Some Things

There are some things you gotta
learn from your mother.
There are some things you'll
learn from the dead.
There are some things you'll
learn from a stranger.
And some things are
better left unsaid.

But no matter who becomes
your teacher,
there are some things
you'll need to survive.
It's best to learn these things
when you're young,
they'll help to keep you alive.

You'll need to learn to read a room,
know exactly where you are.
Be aware of your surroundings,
these words can take you far.

Long Weekend in Vegas

I started yelling at the judge.
She started yelling back at me.
And all I really wanted
was for the law to let me be.

I got a cheap hotel in Vegas.
I got drunk for a couple of days.
But after that long weekend,
my head was a jumbled haze.

Everybody's pissed at something,
every single day of the week.
I'm so pissed right now,
I find it hard to speak.

That's what happens everyday,
when you go out on the street.
Everybody's pissed at something,
every single day of the week.

Can't even fool the dog anymore.
I used to have a knack.
Can't even fool the dog anymore.
I hope I get it back.

I started yelling at the judge.
She started yelling back at me.
And all I really wanted
was for the law to let me be.

Coke Whores, Bar Flies and Ladies of the Night

As soon as the sun went down,
I watched as they took flight.
They started making the rounds,
when day turned into night.

The Coke whores, Bar Flies and
Ladies of the Night

Now don't lump them all together,
'cause that just wouldn't be right.
Some say the clothes they wore fit snugly.
In fact, they were down right tight.

The Coke whores, Bar Flies and
Ladies of the Night

Now years ago, I knew a few
and a few knew me, it's true.
So I won't say a negative word
cuz that wouldn't be the right thing to do.

Now when the sun comes up
it gets scary.
Mascara and face makeup a mess.
I watched the girls come home
in various stages of undress.

Now this happens every morning
and it causes such a fright.
But what else can be expected from
The Coke whores, Bar Flies and
Ladies of the Night.

Old Guy

I became an old guy
seemingly overnight.
First it was my knees,
then it was my sight.
And now it seems that lately,
everyday when I wake up,
something new feels broken,
something new's Fucked up.

⚜⚜⚜⚜⚜⚜

Family deValues

Some of the kindest, nicest, most giving
and intelligent people I've known have
been Atheist Singles. But I never hear
about "Atheist's Values or Single's
Values."

Bad Marketing I guess.

Hospice Nurse

Does the hospice nurse go home and cry
after a day spent helping someone die?
Or does she go home and have a drink
'cause each day is spent on the brink?

If I get a chance before I go,
I'll ask my nurse, 'cause I'd like to know.
How she does it each and every day
no matter the weather, no matter the pay?

Hospice Nurse
what an amazing profession.
Experts, you see, at life's final lesson.

Kindness, compassion,
that's what it takes.
Bring those two traits
and there'll be no mistakes.

W. I. M. P.

Not many people let you
inside of their "shell."
It takes courage. So I guess
on some level, I'm not a
wimp. Anyway, I have a new
acronym for the word.

W onderfully

I maginative

M ulti-faceted

P erson

W. I. M. P.

A "Wimp" Doesn't

A wimp doesn't get up as many times as I did. A wimp doesn't publish his truth, especially when it renders him naked. Society can make you feel negative about yourself if you're not good at confrontation. I've thought of myself as a wimp for this very reason. But a wimp could not accomplish what I have without courage and determination. I have not broken a promise to myself since I quit drinking alcohol, many years ago.

Father/Son

Even the boy who hated him

Became his dad

Along with the boy

who thought it wouldn't happen

to him

Became his dad

Even the boy who was educated

Became his dad

Even the boy who didn't know it

Became his dad

I Hope She's Smart

I have to laugh when I see
women in high heels,
false eye lashes, push up bras
and a come Fuck me dress,
complain about men ogling.
Ya know, when I see
false eyelashes,
heavy eye makeup and
butt crack titty cleavage,
the first thing
I say to myself is,
"I hope she's smart."

The Slave Owners

My behavior toward women, while mostly acceptable back in 1973, would be considered horrendous today and totally unacceptable.

Then again, we've glorified certain slave owners as "great minds" and have built statues to them. We even put them on our money. Why wasn't I taught the truth if the truth was OK? Like, yeah we owned people but ....ya know, a lot of people did.

I made almost every mistake a human being is capable of making. Without honesty, education, direction, guidance, understanding and love, all of us are susceptible to the same behavior as the slave owners.

Sadly, there are many members in the current Republican Party that are quite similar to the slave owners, in that they are both anti-education and anti-truth.

Please Piss in the Cup

Ya know,

there's so much information in your urine,

yet you just keep pissin' it away.

But you better save some for the doctor,

it just may save your life one day.

Don't want to be a mover or a shaker.

Don't want to see my life go that way.

I'd rather just keep doin what I'm doin'.

And hope I don't piss it all away.

Customer Service?

A few years ago, a rude customer
service person at Twinspires
indignantly stated that she
"knows how to talk to old people
'cause I worked in a nursing home."
Ken said,
"You don't work there any more
do you?"
And hung up on her!

Good News/Bad News

The Good News—
There's a cure.

The Bad News—
We need all of your Earthly
possessions and all your
future income to pay for it.

My Hotel California

My hope is that humanity comes up with a better way for old people to leave life than in a nursing home; a civilized and humane way to die.

I would make it open to all the terminally ill, along with people experiencing excruciating chronic pain, instead of this brutal alternative of no assisted suicide.

I'm thinking of something similar to an adult Disneyland, a place where you would be around professionally happy people who would help you down the road to finality. A place where you would check

in but you would never leave.
I realize the Eagles were the first to coin the term "Hotel California" but I think my idea of "Checking Out" might be a little different from theirs. I don't believe death has to be morbid. I believe there should be a bigger celebration on your way out than the one they gave you when you arrived.

Note:
"There are worse things than death."
This is a quote from my good friend former NFL quarterback,
Norris Weese, who was suffering from terminal cancer.

   8/12/1951 - 1/20/1995

The "B" Team

I believe we're all on levels. There are the "A" team superstars who have been that way since birth. Then there are the rest of us. We learn our levels when we're around 8, 9 or 10 years old. I could've been on the "A" team but I would've been a sub. That was little league baseball. I decided back then that I would rather play. So the "B" team was perfect. This level would continue through my entire life. Jobs, women, friends, "B" team. Trust me, there is nothing wrong with being a star on the

"B" Team.

Childhood Friends

It's so easy to make friends as a child. All you need is another child. But as we get older, more and more obstacles get in the way. Like:

Do they Drink?
Do they Smoke Weed?
Do they Smoke Tobacco?
Are they Vegan?
Are they a Religious Nut?
Are they Vaccinated?
Are they Racist?
Are they a Gun Nut?
A Political Nut?

Note: It is probably not wise to send "The Shell Books" to any of the above.

WHY?

I learned when I was very young
that life's not long for everyone
some will live
and some will die
some will laugh
and some will cry

It hasn't changed since time began
every year it starts again

just read the papers and you'll see
it's gonna happen to you and me

I learned when I was very young
that life *is* fair for everyone
but that real fairness doesn't come
until *all* of your life is said and done

The Struggle

Some of me grew up
Some of me grew old

Some of me still thinks
like a twelve year old

It's changed a lot
but it's also stayed the same

As you get a little older
there're just more folks to blame

Life's been a lesson
I've learned grudgingly

but once I learned the lesson
I was set free

Here's the lesson I learned:

Almost nothing
was as important as I made it.

me

I mentioned in
"Crack the Shell Wide Open"
that I wished I was proud
of where I'm from but I'm
not. But I am proud of what
I accomplished after I left.
Every goal was met.
Amends were made
wherever necessary
and possible.
Became a great husband.
Really proud of my writing.
All of it.
Could've drank but didn't.
Could've quit life but didn't.

Trojan Horse

You know they can turn
your lights off
stop your water from running hot

They can take over the
whole country
and all the rights you got

And in this tech world we're
living in
they won't have to fire a shot

I've been calling it a Trojan horse
but there are those who disagree

I think you should take a second
look while all of us are still free

Good Money

What pay level denotes
"Good Money"?
At what denomination does the
job pay
"Good Money"?
You know, he makes
"Good Money,"
he can certainly afford to
pay for that.
By the way, a person knows
what "Good Money" is
even before they make it.
And one of the best thoughts
to go through a person's mind
is this:
"Fuck her, at least I'm still
makin'
"Good Money."

Social Stage Fright

After I quit drinking alcohol, I found I could no longer defend myself, verbally or physically. I never really liked arguing anyway but I could do it drunk. After I stopped drinking, if someone confronted me I'd shrink, wimp like. I became the opposite of what I was as a drinker. **Everything** *changed, especially socially.*
I called it
Social Stage Fright.
Nowadays it's called
Social Anxiety

Shay's Lament

Some of my thoughts are tasteless.
Some of my decisions seem strange.
That might be because
there's a force at work,
a force that I'm trying to change.

I feel it every morning.
It's still there in the afternoon.
I keep hoping I can figure it out,
and I'm hoping it'll be soon.

'Cause
Some of my thoughts are tasteless.
Some of my decisions seem strange.
That might be because
there's a force at work,
a force that I'm trying to change.

Although some of you are concerned,
I promise, there's nothing you can do.
You see, some of the things
that are happening to me,
have nothing to do with you.

cont.

'Cause
Some of my thoughts are tasteless.
Some of my decisions seem strange.
That might be because
there's a force at work,
a force that I'm trying to change.

Now, I'm sorry if my decisions hurt you.
'Cuz that's not what I'm trying to do.
I'm just trying to figure out who I am
and what I'm supposed to do.

'Cause
Some of my thoughts are tasteless.
Some of my decisions seem strange.
That might be because
there's a force at work,
a force that I'm trying to change.

Beer Muscles

You get them when you drink.
Beer Muscles
They make you stronger,
so you think.
Beer Muscles
Stop drinking, they go away.
Beer Muscles
I found this out
when I put the beer away.
Beer Muscles
Without them you're so weak.
Beer Muscles
Do you know of what I speak?
Beer Muscles
It's not like it was before.
Beer Muscles
I don't have them anymore.
Beer Muscles

Weekend in Boston

Coke vile in hand,
we ordered black and tan.
Together,
we crawled the Freedom Trail.

It's Boston, you see
and boy, I gotta pee.
This sure will be a day
to remember.

Though the memories are vague,
we remember these days
and the fun we had
runnin' the streets.

My wife and I were young
but when all was said and done,
we learned exactly
what history had to teach.

Now, we don't remember much.
But that's the special touch.
The highlights
seem to float in mid air.

How we made the drive
and managed to stay alive?
We must have angels
that really do care.

Again

These killings again,
so obscene.
Doing nothing again,
so it seems.
More scars that can't be seen,
too many know what I mean.

*This **IS** who we are.*
*We are **NOT** better than this.*
Get angry?
It does no good.
Scream?
I think you should.
***Vote** for this to stop.*
*We **can** make this stop.*
***Vote** for this to stop.*

BIG ONES

I was born with the genitals of a man but the emotions of a woman. It's been a struggle. I cried a lot, young and old. I have way too much compassion for an ordinary male. I'm also extremely sensitive. I cry over nothing. DNA is a bitch. But we're born who we're born, aren't we.

Although I've never wanted to change my body from male to female, it might have been easier for me emotionally if I would've had a vagina.

I had never even heard the term transgender until recently. But it's starting to make sense to me now. Not in the extreme, like those who suffer with gender dysphoria, but over the years, I have identified equally with the feelings of women and men.

In my teens and into my twenties, while I was hitting on girls and women, men were hitting on me. And it wasn't just the fact that I spent a lot of time in the French Quarter. This happened to me in every city I lived in. Had it not been so taboo, I might have even tried sex with a man. Some of the guys were really good looking. I've loved quite a few guys during my life but never physically. I'm grateful that's one thing I don't have to deal with. Remember, I'm a wimp. I can't even imagine how much strength it takes for a gay person to come out.

Daycare

Children owe their parents nothing. Parents have to earn love. Remember, not one child on this earth asked to be here and yet most of you ask them to fulfill *your* dreams.

Quit having children you don't have time for. What we're seeing out of humanity in 2021 is the result of not having a parent at home when school lets out.

Daycare *is* child abuse
and the future will pay.

MS13

It must take unbearable pain and abuse to become a gang member. I can't even imagine the abuse these human beings have experienced on their journey to MS13. It should go without saying that obviously I hate the evil but I understand what created it.

Southern Charm

Quick Temper, Loud Mouth,
just proving every day
that I was raised in the South.

Don't care for strangers,
'cuz "day not from 'round here."
Stay with my kind 'cuz
it's "the other" I fear.

A Waste of Good Weed

If you use alcohol with marijuana, you don't intensify the marijuana, you diminish it. The alcohol overpowers the THC and you get an alcohol high. In other words, you get drunk, not high and it becomes a waste of good weed. This is a good time to quote a great librarian named Cody,
"Alcohol is poison."

There is a difference

When I got sober I realized I didn't know how to talk to "day" women. All of the women I had met over the previous twelve years were "night" women, even if I had met them during the day.

Some Controversial Questions and Comments....

Preoccupied

*Many years ago, a young woman once said to me, "All you think about is sex." I immediately told her that wasn't true. It's just the **first** thing.*

Not So Fast, Sista

Before you criticize anything I write, remember, someone ok'd W.A.P. for network tv. I wonder what the "Me Too" movement thought about the Grammy Awards performance of W.A.P? Along with educating men and boys, you probably should educate girls and women, too.

Titty Meat

What's up with women exposing
their breasts every chance they get?
Although this is certainly not a
completely new phenomenon,
it seems that it's become a thing.
However, cleavage's similar
appearance to
"plumbers crack"
should be of real concern.

Plumbers Crack

When you look closely, you can
hardly tell the difference:
Is it "Titty cleavage?"
Or "Plumbers crack?"

2021 The Year of the Cleavage

This trend seemed to come upon us

over the last year or so.

It reminds me of the 2 day shadow

that was hip for men a couple of years ago.

I've never seen so much cleavage.

Even women with no breasts

are wearing jackets

with no blouse or undershirt

to show off their concave.

What's up with this?

Some cleavage is ugly, really ugly,

like butt crack ugly.

But nobody has the nerve to tell you.

I just did.

I might just be the only **real** friend

you have.

One Last Controversial Question on this subject:

Would Harvey Weinstein, that sleazy Motherfucker, be in jail today if he looked like a young Warren Beatty or Brad Pitt?

This is an honest book and this is a fair question. Maybe the answer is "Yes, you bet he would," but it's still something to think about.

Good Luck, Y'all

A man and a woman have sex.
A lot of the time they are
drunk or **high.**
Nine months later you pop out.
They may be good people,
full of **love.**
They may be bad people,
full of **shit.**
They now control everything in your
life for eighteen years.
what you will believe,
what you will eat,
who you will associate with.
They control how you look,
how you dress, everything!
Then you grow up and
re-gift the same thing.
Good Luck!

Good Sex

*I've always found it hard to believe
the friends of mine who said
that they never masturbated.
My body masturbated for me the
1st time.
I took care of all the others.
It was easy.
I know what I like.*

Fucking or Making Love?

I've never really liked calling sex
"making love."
The naked stuff is Fucking.
If it's any good.
I believe you "make love"
with your clothes on.
How you treat each other with your
clothes on is what
"making love" really is.

More about the 1970's

I personally knew **many** women who enjoyed being **sex objects** when I was younger. Don't get me wrong, I completely understand what women are saying today. My only point is that the majority of the women that crossed **my** path, said nothing and even encouraged me. It took women over 2000 years to say enough is enough. Don't blame the older generation of men for something that was taught, accepted and in some cases expected. If boys growing up now act like that, throw the book at 'em.

White Girl Twerkin'

White girl twerkin'
but somethin' ain't workin'
what the hell she tryin' to do?

White girl twerkin'
butt cheeks jerkin'
Start to turn 'em black and blue

She's workin' so hard
But somethins' not right
SHE can't be twerkin'
'Cause dem butt cheeks too
white

White girl twerkin'
but somethin' ain't workin'
what the hell she tryin' to do?

Better Late than Never

I honestly did not know that some of my treatment of women years ago was abhorrent.

Little boys look up to the big boys, the men. We also watched the reaction of the women. I learned it from the elders. That behavior was everywhere.

Now, I know better. It's good to see that boys and young men of today are being shown a different way.

MAGA Military

Ret. US Army LTG Michael Flynn said he didn't call for a coup.
He called for a cootchie, cootchie coo.

—

K C

Pundit Poop

I'd be remiss if I didn't say something about
smug and pompous,
 privilege poster boy,
Rick Santorum.
You better go to confession, you bastid!
We didn't bring civilization to America,
but we sure did end a few.

❧❧❧❧❧❧❧

It's Impossible?
Don't tell me it's impossible to
change the Constitution. We've
already removed
"the pursuit of happiness,"
from the
Declaration of Independence.

The American Religions
You mean, no one's religion told
them slavery was wrong?

Believe it or Not

Being a bartender in New Orleans
afforded me the opportunity to
witness some pretty
bizarre behavior.
But for the life of me,
I cannot understand the
whole Kimberly Guilfoyle thing.

Let's Throw the Book at 'em

Republicans seem to be more like
Old Testament God,
Angry, Punishing, Judgmental.

Democrats seem to be more like
New Testament God,
Caring for all with Kindness.

Origins

Stories told by people who thought
the world was flat.
Told in a language that no longer
exists.
Relayed by word of mouth or oral
history by people who couldn't
read or write.
Christianity was ordered by a King to
be the only religion people could
believe in.
Not a God, a Fucking King!
Don't you see any holes in that story?
They didn't even have Fucking paper.
They had Papyrus.
Did ya ever try to erase something
on papyrus?

If you're one of the people who
believes the Bible is the direct
word of God and nothing
has been changed from the
oral history to the printed word,
you haven't heard my wife
tell a story.

Fearful Bunch

For people who are supposedly "saved,"
Christians are the most fearful people
that I've known on Earth.

Fear God
Fear Change
Fear Liberals
Fear Brown People
Fear Immigrants
Fear Black people
Fear Socialists
Fear Fear Fear fear

Dear Christians, even the people who
don't agree with you are just like you.
They're afraid of something, too. Is it so
hard to get along with people who just
happen to disagree with you? You have
to admit the stories are **kinda bizarre.**

I was under the impression that belief in
God was intended to make people
better, kinder and more caring.

Manna

I remember reading about manna in the Old Testament but I don't know anyone who eats it anymore. In fact, I don't know anyone that's ever eaten it. I've checked around and I've never even seen manna on a menu. I even asked at Trader Joes. They looked at me as if I was crazy.

If manna were real, don't you think we would at least see it in soul food? Like ham hocks and manna or collard greens and manna? If not soul food, definitely Cajun food. You know, deep fried manna or manna etouffee. Cajuns eat almost anything.

Now I realize the story is about trusting God but if you've ever been hungry, I think you can see Moses' side too.

Amen, Brotha

Middle Ground

There is no middle ground when it comes to racism. Middle ground for a racist was Jim Crow. So what do we do? Continue to condemn it. Point out how costly it is and remind the racists that it's better to live with others as best you can because you can't kill all the people you hate.

Mixed Race?
If you believe the stories in the Bible, aren't we all mixed race by now? We all share Human blood.

The New Republican Party
I love watching EVIL eat EVIL

January 6th

I grew up with the insurrectionists.
I wasn't one of them
but I knew them all.
I was raised with the insurrectionists.
They were my neighbors one and all.

Some of these folks seem to have been
born with hate,
holdovers from an ugly past.
I've never really been sure
what they've been pissed about
and I was always too afraid to ask.

Jan 6th didn't surprise me.
I've been waiting to see this for years.
And not much has changed
since I was a kid,
to alleviate those fears.

I grew up with the insurrectionists.
I wasn't one of them
but I knew them all.
I was raised with the insurrectionists.
They were my neighbors one and all.

Original Sin

What would you do
if they'd done it to you
or to people who carried **your** name?

Would you just "let it go"
'cause it was "so long ago"
or would you look for someone
to blame?

And when you found out,
would you just scream and shout?
No, I think you'd want to do
them the same.

But you can change your
life's course.
Get off your high horse.
And admit we should all
share in the shame.

INFRASTRUCTURE

A WORD THEY USE IN
WASHINGTON, DC.
NO ONE KNOWS WHAT IT MEANS BUT
IT'S EVEN GIVEN A WEEK FROM
TIME TO TIME.

The teachings of Jesus Christ
or a vote
for d rump.
Faith in Practice or Hypocrisy?

Twice impeached, one term ex-president
d rump was asked about his
convictions.
His answer was that he hadn't even
been charged yet and other than that,
he had no convictions.

This could be costly

It seems that lately my wife and I
have been voting for things that will
probably cost us higher taxes.
I have no problem with lifting
ALL the boats.

⚜ ⚜ ⚜ ⚜ ⚜ ⚜

White Only?

I just watched fifty year old
Phil Michelson win the 2021 PGA
tournament by two strokes, which
was double the amount of **black**
people at the tournament.
But America is not a racist country?

Acts of God

Most, if not all of the terrible
natural events that occur are
called "Acts of God" and yet
people still worship this God.
If that's not indoctrination,
I don't know what is.

Honorable People

Just remember, it's the people **you**
consider good enough to represent **your**
district and country that got us into this
mess. Not the artists, not the musicians,
not the factory workers,
but rather the so-called
"Honorable People"
that keep this mess going.
Racist politicians, naive politicians,
ambitious politicians, dishonest
politicians that **you** elect.

Ya Think?

Ya think Mitch Mc Connell has ever used the
N word?
Ya think Mitch Mc Connell has ever used the
N word?
Ya think Mitch Mc Connell has ever used the
N word?
Ya think Mitch Mc Connell has ever used the
N word?
Ya think Mitch Mc Connell has ever used the
N word?
Ya think Mitch Mc Connell has ever used the
N word?
Ya think Mitch Mc Connell has ever used the
N word?
Ya think Mitch Mc Connell has ever used the
N word?
Ya think Mitch Mc Connell has ever used the
N word?
Ya think Mitch Mc Connell has ever used the
N word?
Ya think Mitch Mc Connell has ever used the
N word?
Ya think Mitch Mc Connell has ever used the
N word?
Yes, and J think he still does. Grrrrr

My Home Town

I think 90% of the people I was raised
with/around were racists. In order to survive,
the other 10% just kept their mouths shut.
They were too outnumbered to speak up.

**You ever notice how Republicans
always feel that the "people"
are trying to
"get over" on the country?**

d rump's America

It's no longer necessary to make friends.
It's now only necessary to make money.

Most of the *cruel* people I have
known during my lifetime have been
religious.

And remember, you can't spell
religion without the
EGO.

He Said What?

On what subject, other than religion, do you allow someone to tell you remarkably bizarre stories and instead of suggesting psychological help, you think of them as *wise?*

I asked my religious friends to check and see if they can get a weekend pass to come down and see me after we die.

What are you gonna do when both sides believe God is on their side?

Global Warming

Whatcha gonna do
when the heat keeps risin'?
Whatcha gonna do to beat the heat?
Whatcha gonna do if
the food keeps dyin'?
What the hell ya gonna eat?

Global Warming
Flooding the streets
Global Warming
What the hell ya gonna eat?

Now here come the robots
to make life easier, they say.
But what will regular people do,
when all the jobs go away?

Global warming
Flooding the streets
Global Warming
What the hell ya gonna eat?

Young couples havin' babies.
They want a family, they say.
But what will their children do,
  if the robots get their way?

Global Warming
What the hell ya gonna do?
Global Warming
it's up to me, it's up to you.

Hurricanes getting bigger,
treating houses like they were sticks.
The really sad thing about it,
it's still something we can fix.

Global Warming
Flooding the streets
Global Warming
What the hell ya gonna eat?

American Justice

I need to paraphrase something I heard on The Daily Show with Trevor Noah. If you kill one person you go to jail for life but if you're responsible for thousands, even millions of deaths, you get a book tour.

I have not forgiven George W. Bush for Iraq and I will never forgive the people who voted for d rump a second time.

Mass Shootings

Maybe we need to arm God.
I guess I just didn't realize that Jesus taught
so much **hate and bigotry.**

Wisdom

*Another reason I no longer believe in a
benevolent God is that wisdom
only comes to most of us right before death.
Yes, I blame the Creator for that.*

A Better Way

I believe you can teach humility without the bizarre stories.
There has to be a better way than mainstream religion.

⚜⚜⚜⚜⚜⚜

Yin and Yang

There's even a yin and yang of Kennedy's.
The ones from Massachusetts and that toothless lunatic from Louisiana.

⚜⚜⚜⚜⚜⚜

80 Rich People

I'm really tired of hearing this next question: How can this happen in the richest country in the world? They call us the richest country in the world because we have 80 of the richest people in the world. There's one problem, no, actually there's 80.

They don't share.

White Man's World

I was raised in a white man's world.

Where life was set for a woman or a girl.

No choices given for what she would do.

She was born to cook and clean for you.

Although this life took some

pressure away,

it could sure be boring in the day to day.

But the real injustice was that

she had no say.

She was told when to work.

And she was told when to play.

That's the way it was when I came up.

If you weren't a white man

then you'd better shut up.

I was raised in a white man's world.

Fifties Girls

Blame June Cleaver and women like her. The ones that didn't say a thing. As you can see, men ARE teachable.
We just needed women to teach us. But June did seem happy, really happy, cooking, cleaning and dressing up.

Everyone is not a mover and a shaker.

So Far Anyway

d rump has shown people that they can be assholes and get away with it.

So far anyway

Just Kill 'em All

Maybe people who disagree with you
shouldn't be allowed to live

Maybe people who disagree with you should
be introduced to the shiny shiv

Maybe people who disagree with you should
die an ugly death

Maybe people who disagree with you should
immediately be laid to rest

Maybe that's how extreme you've gotten

Looks like decency has been forgotten

Seems like the whole damn world

is rotten

But ya know, you can't kill em all

or have you forgotten

Hitler tried

but he got gotten

The New Confederacy

While I don't believe the

"South will rise again,"

I do believe it can explode again.

Racism + Religiosity + Gun Rights =

BOOM, BANG, BOOM!

Don't act like you're shocked

when it happens.

RON DESANTIS FOR PRESIDENT

MAKE AMERICA STUPID AGAIN

JUST CALL HIM "MASA!"

The Vote

The 74,222,958 reasons
I've been sad most of my life.
I've been surrounded by d rump
supporters. Sadly, this type of thinking has
been around since this country began.
What's really sad is that they voted for him
even **AFTER** he showed us who he was.
Still optimistic?

Representative Government

If you really want a cabinet that
represents America,
you'd have to appoint
racists to half the positions.

Cable News

I've started thinking of cable news shows
as if they were doors in a fun arcade.
Choose which doors will thrill you the most.
Choose a reality and they'll tell you what
you want to hear.

Naked

I'd like to see what people would
be like if they all had to be naked
for a week.
All talk shows,
Naked
Game shows,
Naked
Ted Cruz at the airport,
Naked
The whole panel on ABC,
Naked
Chris Christie,
Naked
Donna Shalala,
Naked
Let's see what they say,
when they're
Naked
Every show,
except The View.
No, especially The View

Naked

Faith

I stood back and looked at the people who believed and the people who didn't. The people who didn't seemed more like me. During my lifetime, I took a good hard look at believers and non-believers.
The non-believers in general are better educated than the believers. They also were less prejudiced, less fearful and less judgmental.

No Higher Level

I am very grateful to the brave men and women who have worn the uniform of our country with honor and have died for my right to write and publish this book. I openly admit that I do not possess the type of courage that they possess. Although there are many different levels of courage, risking one's life for another is the highest.

Me too

I was wanted at times
but not loved.
I was used at times
but not loved.
I was not loved for most of
my life.

KC

Small Life?

You could have been kind
and enlarged it.
Kindness = Success

I miss the slow world.

A Tale of 2 Cities

There were 2 cities that I lived in during my travels where the people had no souls, Las Vegas, Nevada and Washington, DC. There's actually a caste system that exists in Washington, DC. It's based on your formal education.

1. Ivy league- most desired
2. Military academy
3. Big name sports university (e.g. Notre Dame, Penn State, or Duke)

Next came:

4. Any state university

Followed by:

5. Jr college
6. High school
7. GED- (just keep sweeping)

I found that the "educated elite" do as much to destroy unity in America as that idiot Marjorie Taylor Green.

My Grain

I always knew my mind was different than most of the people I met or loved or associated with. Most minds don't go to the place my mind does. I'm honestly not sure why this happens. You're kinda stuck with the mind you're born with.

My depression seems to be similar to what I've heard about migraine headaches. I'm not depressed every day, I have episodes. Many people who don't suffer from depression don't understand it. My depression hibernates from time to time but it is also very patient. I've suffered from depression since the age of seven. It has waxed and waned through the years but it never goes away. Sometimes it's months before it returns from hiatus but it's been with me for as long as I can remember.

There was no such thing as "Clinical Depression" when I was young. The only treatment was ridicule.

Brotherly What?

*My older brother treats me the way
our father did but uses bigger words.
In fact, in over 60 years of adulthood,
my older brother has never called
to just say "hi." Not once.*

Brotherly Love

*As an adult, I can't remember being
angry at my brothers. Hurt, yes, but
no anger, I know who raised them.
I also don't have a memory of my
older brother ever asking me how I
was doing in my whole life. We are all
so damaged but as far as I know, I'm
the only one to talk about it.*

BROTHER BIG WORDS

He's just like his father,
rigid and cold.
He's never been kind to me,
when young or when old.
Brother Big Words
He's the smartest you see,
so much smarter than me.
His start was fast,
mine has been slow.
He finished college, I didn't,
you know.
It's the story that never changes.
No matter how many times
you turn the pages.
(And it doesn't even matter
what you turn out to be).
Brother Big Words
50 cents or a dollar.
That's what people pay
for the Big Words they use,
for the Big Words they say.
Brother Big Words
Kindness, not a Big Word.
Love, just one syllable
that says so much.
Seems too simple for
Brother Big Words.
Could it be that he relies on
Big Words too much?

Important Note:

I want to explain a little about why I talk about everything, the embarrassing stuff as well as the painful stuff. I do it because just as I know there are other alcoholics, there are other people who are estranged from their family or just have an unhealthy family dynamic in general. You are not alone, not unlike my AA brothers and sisters. And I also know that you can survive. Just because you came out of the same vagina doesn't necessarily mean you will be compatible. Like my friend Levi Simmons used to say,

"It be dat way sometimes."

Very Important Additional Note:

Levi died in his attic of a heart attack as he tried to escape the rising flood waters of Hurricane Katrina. He was an older black man who treated me like his younger brother. I miss you Levi.

Ruff, Ruff, Ruff, Grrrrrr

*Anytime a woman was strong and called
me on my bullshit, she won. Smart and
strong disarm me. In fact, when anyone
called me on my bullshit, they won.
I've always been all bark.
But very loud barking
can be intimidating,
especially if you don't know
the dog very well.*

Trouble

When I was young, I got into trouble
for NOT telling the truth.
Now that I'm older, I'm getting in
trouble for the exact opposite.

Hate the ABUSE not the ABUSER

ABUSERS have usually
been ABUSED themselves
I ABUSED in the same way my
father ABUSED,
LOUD
Hell, I didn't even consider it
ABUSE
for years
I would only take advantage of a
smaller size person
Notice I didn't specify women
only someone weaker
Nothing physical
only loud and intimidating

I'd go Mike Ditka Crazy
Just like my daddy did

Only Human

You know, I'm not ashamed to be human.

That's how I wake up every day.

No, I'm not ashamed to be human.

That's who we are, they say.

Acknowledge that you are human.

Do better, you know that you can.

But don't be ashamed to be human.

It's the best part of livin' man.

Mistakes that are long forgiven

by the dead and even some of the livin'

will all turn to dust

'cause people don't rust,

while all of us hope we're forgiven.

JULIE, JULIE, JULIE

Julie would've made the perfect sister. I talk a lot about being a wimp and not handling confrontation well. I would easily risk pain and death to fight for a sister like Julie. Julie just appeared one day. She was the spark that made "The Shell Books" possible. She merely liked one of my poems and told me so. Her simple act of kindness has helped to make my life more meaningful.

Thank you, Julie

Please Support Greenpeace

If it Keeps on Rainin'

I believe we all have a reservoir where sadness goes. That reservoir seems to be a different size in everyone. Some overflow immediately upon disappointment. Then there are those larger reservoirs that seemingly can hold back anything. But don't be deceived. Pain and sorrow both need a place to go or even the deepest reservoir will eventually overflow.

Heartfelt Music

Can't stand the heartfelt music.
Those strings broke long ago.
Now they try to sell us decency
with violin and piano.

Here comes the speaker.
Who really cares?
Now, what's the ask?
Oh, aren't you aware?

Send us your money.
We need it bad.
We're the best friend
that you never had.

So send them your money.
'Cuz they've pulled those strings.
That heartfelt music,
oh, how it stings.

Can't stand the heartfelt music.
Those strings broke long ago.
Now they try to sell us decency,
with violin and piano.

The Player

I was the player till I got played
did all the work but didn't get paid
seems my talents had started to fade
I used to be the one that
always got laid
but lately things have
started to change
my life it seems has been rearranged
I was the player till I got played
that's when it all seemed to
get so strange
no matter what I said
it got misconstrued
more times than not it came out
sounding rude
Boy how things change as the years
go rushing by
I'd completely lost my touch
but I wasn't sure why
it seems it just happens
there's really nothing you can do
Truth is getting laid was never
up to you
I was the player till I got played

Teardrops

Although you've never seen
my tears,
I'm sure yours look the same.
'Cause tears don't care
what face they use
and they rarely know your name.

They don't need to know your name.
They don't care what
made them flow.
The reason,
even your tears may never know.

So before you judge
a teardrop harshly,
remember what I've said.
Don't put your teardrops up for trial.
In fact, just go to bed.

This is a piece I call

Gun *penis*

Gun *penis*
Gun *penis*
Gun *penis*

Corvette *penis*
Corvette *penis*
Corvette *penis*

Beer Drinkers or Pot Smokers

Beer drinkers seem to buy guns
Pot smokers seem to buy cakes
A news report from CNN
(the year 2041)

Last night, at a gathering on the South side, a mass caking took place. This was the third mass caking in the last month. We'll have footage at eleven but I'll try to describe the scene as best I can.

I have to be honest, I've been to quite a few mass cakings in the last year and this one tops them all. I guess you could say it "takes the cake."

As soon as I got to the scene, I realized this was big. Icing, filling, cake, **everywhere.** The sidewalk was covered with whipped cream. Multi-colored sprinkles covered the lawn. I have never seen anything like this.

I spoke to one of the victims briefly.
This is all he could say, "We were all
asked to bring our cakes. It was
advertised as a peaceful gathering of
cake lovers. Then out of the blue, a
cake lands on my head. It could've
been an accident but it caused me to
fall back in my chair, which caused
the cake that was in **my** lap to take
flight. It was then, all hell broke loose.
And I'll tell you something else, it
wasn't just cakes. Pies, pastries,
almost anything containing whipped
cream."

We were outside when he told me
his story and cautioned me that the
inside was even worse. As I walked
through the debris, I could hear some
people laughing. I even thought I
heard someone having sex.

You know, my father was a reporter
back in the day and I remember him
telling stories of the mass shootings
of **his** time. The main difference
between the shootings that my

father's generation experienced, is that no one dies at the cakings. And the floors are covered with multi-colored icing instead of blood.

NOTE: In conclusion, **it IS possible** to end gun violence. It will be difficult but **it IS possible** to amend the Constitution.

Maybe one day, the only thing parents will have to worry about when their children leave to go out for the evening is the cleaning bill.

We don't need more guns America

but we can always use more cake.

Would you still be proud to be White?

Would you still be proud to be white
if your grandpa was there that night?
When the boys dragged that
Black man out of his car.
You know, all the boys from the local bar.
When they tied that rope 'round his neck,
would you still say what the heck?
Would you still be proud to be white
if your grandpa was there that night?
When all the boys from the bar dragged
that **Black** man out of his car.
Would you still be proud to be white
when they strung him up that night
and left his body there
to swing in the breeze?
And now you're a carrier of this
racist disease.
And if your grandpa was there,
would you even care?

cont.

Would you still be proud to be white
when you learned
the truth from that night?
'Cause I'm not proud to be white.
No, not tonight.
And I've heard that sick joke
about my being woke,
but I know in my heart
that I'm right.
So now it's time to decide
shine a light on the truth
or continue to hide.
Would you still be proud to be white?

Dark Side

If you take the time and
look close enough
I'm certain you will see
everyone has a dark side
That's including you and me

If someone you meet seems pius
it's certain in time you'll find
There are times when even the pius
Act like a big behind

It's just the way that life is
There's not much you can do
And now that you know
you can't change them
How 'bout changing you?

Water, Water Everywhere

I thought I was in love
with every girl I met
and that they would soon
be in love with me

and when I'd get one
to love me back
I'd try to get two
maybe three

Now I didn't invent biology
or 1973
but I thought I was in love
with every girl I met
and they would soon
be in love with me

now before you judge me harshly
I ask you to stop and think
If you were hot and the water
was plenty
would you just take one drink?

little girl Grown Up

She's a little girl grown up
Push up bra and face makeup
And a dirty mouth that won't shut up
But you knew her as a kid

She got her nose pierced
you know, her friends did too
and at 15 years old
she got her first tattoo

So you weren't even a little surprised
when she walked up to you and said
hey big fella,
would you like to go to bed?

I took a step back
I needed a moment to think
I called the bartender
and ordered another drink

By the time I turned around
To answer her query
My morality kicked in
And I'd become a little leery

But luckily for me
She was on to another
I would've said no thank you
I had dated her grandmother

The Girls and the Women

Some were fun
Some were serious
Some were so good looking
I couldn't resist

Some pissed me off
Some hurt me deeply
Some were my lovers
so indiscreetly

Some I would hide from
Some hid from me
And there were some
That just wouldn't let me be

Some were fun
Some were serious
Some were so good looking
I couldn't resist

Gentlemen's Clubs

*I've never enjoyed watching beautiful
women dance suggestively, especially if I
can't grab one, pin her down and
Fuck her silly.
I guess I just don't see the art!*

Rare Breed

I am a heterosexual man who likes
ballads, theater, performance art,
music, dance, poetry
and having sex with women.
I don't like:
Hunting- too bloody
Fishing-too slimy
Carpentry- too dirty
Cage boxing- too brutal

And I never did get Gentlemen's Clubs.

Coyotes at 3:15

If you live around some, you know what I mean.
What's all the racket?
Why do you scream?
This is the question for coyotes at 3:15.

Now, it's better than gunshots
or hearing the neighbors fight.
My question to coyotes is,
why 3:15 at night?

They came in the middle of a dream,
coyotes at 3:15.
And now that I'm awake,
I'm kinda glad.

It was that cliff dream,
where you're about to fall.
But the coyotes woke me
with their terrifying call.

I wasn't happy at first.
I think everyone knows why.
It's loud and it's scary
when coyotes start to cry.

Coyotes at 3:15.
Sometimes your dreams
are not what they seem.
They're just coyotes at 3:15.

Cigarettes and Jim Crow

Where did all the time go
since cigarettes were cool
and the rule was Jim Crow?

I was just a little boy,
too young to even know,
the evil that existed,
in the smoke and Jim Crow.

"Day got day own beach."
That's what the old men say.
"It may change
but it ain't changin' today."

"Day should stay with day people.
Day should stay with day kind.
It's worked for hundreds of years.
In fact, it's worked just fine."

"Hey man, you got a cigarette?"
"Yeah, I got a new pack."
It was many years
before I started to hack.

Nicotine stained fingers.
Nicotine stained shirts.
cont.

434

Burn holes in everything
and a smell that's much worse.

You better go on 'round back
if your skin is **black.**
You can smoke in the bar all night
but only if your skin is white.

I thought it was important
that all of you should know,
what a bad idea they were:
Cigarettes and Jim Crow.

I was just a little boy,
too young to even know,
the evil that existed,
in the smoke and Jim Crow.

New Title/Same Poop

Most everyone in life gets a chance at a new title. You know, like you're the new general manager, senior White House reporter or like being Knighted.

Sir Elton John- New Title/Same Poop

General Manager- New Title/Same Poop

Executive Director-New Title/Same Poop

Mr President-New Title/Same Poop

Now, if the new title changes your income and the new income changes your diet, maybe your poop won't be the same.

Most assuredly it will still stink.

Unknown Artist/Unknown Writer

If you were alive when
Vincent van Gogh
painted and he gave you one
of his paintings as a gift,
would you have hung it on your
wall so you and your friends
could talk about it and enjoy it?
Or would you just put it in
your closet?

Bourbon Street

Being a bartender in the French Quarter caused eyes to grow in the back of my head. There was a time I could spot an asshole 50 yards away. It was like a sixth sense.

The human voice is similar to silverware. Sometimes it can cut like a knife, other times it can soothe like a spoonful of hot soup on a cold winter's day.

What's up with stick bugs?

If you've never seen a stick bug you should try to see one before you die and wonder.

In the Navy

When I came of age, the only people who got tattoos were usually drunk or in the Navy. Now young people actually make appointments to get drawn on.

To all the conservatives who don't
want to teach
sex education in schools;
Have you ever seen the internet?

Every generation has its own
seemingly insurmountable hill.
Some make it over that hill,
some don't.

COVID-19 Good News

1. No more phony handshakes
2. No holding hands to pray
3. No embarrassing hugs
4. No more doubt as to who the assholes are

I love the Grateful Dead.
But I've always wondered who told Jerry
Garcia he could make a living
with his singing?

Fess Parker

Davy Crockett or Daniel Boone?
It was confusing.

Mental Illness

Health insurance doesn't cover mental
illness. That's crazy!

I always pull for the underdog.
No matter what!

Boy, I sure looked good for a minute.
Too bad the race was two minutes long.

As much as I disliked life,
I hope I'm sad when I die.
That would mean I was finally doing well.

You know how when you dance,
it feels good even if it might look stupid?
I write with that feeling.
If you like writing, write.
It's really none of your business what other
people think of it.

Comic Relief

There are 5 entertainers that make me
think AND laugh.
Bill Hicks, George Carlin, Robin Williams,
Jim Jefferies and Bill Burr.
That's my list.

A Special Thank You to the "Serious People"

*I'd like to thank ALL of the
"Serious People."
I'm not one of you but the older I get,
I can see the need for
"Serious People."*

*My parents didn't know shit and were
afraid of everything. How about yours?*

Forgiveness

There's a real simple way
I think life should work.
Be as kind as you can
and try not to be a jerk.
Learning forgiveness
is an important thing to do.
'Cause if there's one thing that is
certain, one day you'll need it, too.

College Obscenity

I'll never understand how
Nick Saban (9.1 million)
or
Dabo Sweeney (8.3 million)
can even look at themselves in the mirror.
There are others but these are the two
that got stuck in my craw
before I had it removed.

Good Luck and Bad Luck
are pretty much the same.
They just happen.

Bad Habits?
Certain people throughout the
course of my life have questioned
why I bet the horses.
How many people can claim they
have something to look forward
to every twenty minutes?

Trendy

If you continually follow trends, you'll
never start anything. And you will only
know what everyone else knows
and nothing more.

New Orleans

If you look past the facade
you will find
the ugliness of racism
outweighs all of the merriment.
I didn't leave New Orleans because of
black people.

Racism

I've heard it called
America's Original Sin.
It's more like America's Continual Sin.

I become addicted to anything that
makes me feel better than I did before I
did whatever it is.
I like feeling good.

WHY SHOULDN'T I COMBINE SILLY WITH SERIOUS? THAT'S WHAT LIFE IS.

I heard someone say, "Now, I'm dating myself."
And I thought of how I dated myself for years.
Sadly, it was only for the sex.

Cultural Appropriation

I think I've been guilty of appropriating
everything at one time or another.
What about you?
Isn't the United States itself
Cultural Appropriation?

I've been totally broke on more than one
occasion. There's actually something very
peaceful about having nothing else to lose.

No one really knows how human life began or
when. Their egos tell them they know
but they don't.

Everything is generational.
No Myrna's, Murial's or Mildred's
being born today.

There's usually only one "caveat."
For some reason they don't socialize with
the "other" words.

Her Sinful Ways

A young woman in New Orleans once told me
that Fucking is not a sin if you don't enjoy it.
She then admitted to me that she was
indeed a sinner.

447

Ya Never Know

You should be kind to everyone.
Some people you meet can destroy you.

Most of the "so called" great leaders were
drinking brandy for courage.
Do it sober, Winston!

If you have enough, you have enough.
The most important thing a parent can do
is to teach happiness.

I recently saw that Spider-Man
met the Pope.
No, It's true. I saw the photograph.
Just a couple of guys in costumes
"cuttin' it up."

Life expectancy has dropped by one year.
The important thing is, which one?
Hope it's not this one.

I've coined a new word for 2020,
GRUMB.
As in, I'm feeling grumb,
so much grief I'm numb.

Never, "Just be yourself."
Please don't believe that shit.
Your mom was wrong.

Marketing is never meant to inform.
Marketing is **always** meant to convince.

We need one mo letta
to make the world betta
lgbtq + w
Wimps are people, too.

I've always had the desire to become a great
philanthropist. Just not the money.

Over the course of my life, I think I've been blamed
for everything at least once. I was with one woman
who actually blamed *ME* for her period.

Sex was **not** the only reason I enjoyed women
when I was young. Other reasons: kindness,
tenderness, conversation, easy going companion
who liked to be silly.

*As long as you pay your taxes, you are not
required to grow up.
Some people might not like it but
Fuck them!*

I realize I'm no Mark Twain.
Actually, I think of myself as his great,
great, great grandson,
little Timmy Twain.

Yeah, I smoked when I was young and yes,
I developed COPD. So I guess when I die you
can say I phlegmed out. Not only disgusting
but really hard to spell.

Three months before he died, my father said
he finally figured out how to beat the horses.
Pancreatic Cancer.

I went to 3 different high schools and didn't
pay much attention. I went to one semester
of college and didn't pay attention at all.
My writing comes from just plain
paying attention.

A New York Minute?
*It only takes a minute for a minute to disappear
and once that minute disappears you can never
get it back.
And it only takes a minute.*

After 50 years of relationships I'm still not
sure if it's easier to live with someone
smarter than me or someone who is not as
smart as me.
Certainly there are challenges with both.

I've believed for a long time that
some courage is overrated.
Example:
When a golf announcer whispers,
"that was a courageous shot."

Robot Office Memo:

People cost money.
We don't need any more people.
Recharge and immediately return
to your designated area.
Thank You.

Cigarettes...
The reason I can no longer
smoke weed.
Fuck cigarettes!
Yet another lie takes its toll.

I have one important question
for the future.
What will the regular people do?

Do Jack Rabbits have sex with
regular bunnies?
Do they find them attractive?
Is it socially accepted?

K C

Are Russians the original rednecks?

And now, some One Liners or a little more
Edgy Mark Twain

If anything comes before your art,
it's a hobby.
K C

Criticism can kill you or it can be your jet fuel.

K C

The COVID-19 catastrophe is proof that
we shouldn't have let 1957 run 2020.

Can you count all the times that you lied?

Boy, that gravity sure is a double edged sword.

Functional codependency = Happy marriage

"The only person I'm better than is the person I used to be."

AA speaker

Quick Temper

Learned behavior, DNA or both?

If you continue to sweep everything uncomfortable under the rug, eventually you will have a mountain to climb.

Urban Rule Book

People born after 1970 will no longer
be required to say "thank you."

I would've made a good **black** grandma
'cause
I just won't let you quit.

Hallmark Holiday
It's a Hallmark Holiday,
You have no choice!

At any time you wish, you can become
something that you're not.

The Outside World

I KNOW THEY'RE GONNA GET THROUGH
SOONER OR LATER BUT I'M TRYING TO STAVE
THEM OFF.

❀❀❀❀❀❀

Respect your children,
unless they try to eat you.

❀❀❀❀❀❀

I was Biblically high for all of my 20's.

❀❀❀❀❀❀

That laughter really brings up the phlegm!

❀❀❀❀❀❀

Just because you can,
doesn't mean you should.

❀❀❀❀❀❀

Don't feel bad if you're not good looking,
you're normal.

Before you have children, ask yourselves,
"What will they do for a living?"

*I never knew I liked black coffee
till I ran out of milk.*

My wife
If she was just the things I hate about her,
we wouldn't still be together.

*Ghosting says more about the ghoster
than the ghosted.*

If things aren't bad,
you don't know how good you have it.

*We're heading toward a virtual world where
people will only get in the way.*

If life is a gift, is sex an attempt to re-gift?

Keep your judgments to
your own shoes
'cause you've never walked in mine.

Old People Talk

How those apples workin' for ya?

Sometimes we know things that we didn't know we knew and it takes someone else to point that out.

Absolutely, Nobody is a Nobody.

Ghosting is a classless act used by
insecure and fearful people.

Everyone I've known had a dark side.

Had I addressed the racism I was
surrounded by head on,every time it rose
it's ugly head,
I wouldn't be writing today.

*I've come to believe that every pundit on TV
was once a federal prosecutor.*

If you only follow the news that's been
filtered, you will not know what's going on.

Acceptable behavior is generational.

If life is a gift, why does the giver
require us to give it back?

It's not ALL good.

Most people are addicted to their beliefs.

Almost anyone can learn but not
everyone thinks.

How have epaulets survived
all these years?

*I've been called a pussy so many times,
you'd think I'd need a tampon
five days a month.*

461

*If you died today, would you be OK with
the way you lived your life?*

The future is almost guaranteed to
show you just how petty you've been.

*Most people wish they were more
important.*

Important People
*I learned many years ago that you're making
a big mistake if you think the only
important people are the
"Important People."*

Your children owe you nothing but the
respect you give them.

I've come to believe that you can learn a lot more from regular people, than you will from the famous ones.

It's obvious to me that the guys who signed the Constitution would expect us to change the rules and regulations as the muskets became automatic weapons.

Why aren't we past saying things are "dope?"

OPEC may control the oil but WOMEN control the most important of natural resources.

Have you ever wanted something that you knew you couldn't get?

There is a resilience that comes
with rejection.

THE SAMING OF AMERICA

HOW are you GOING TO SING ABOUT
LIFE IN THE COUNTRY,
WHEN everyone HAS BroaDBAND?

Honesty is Love.

Bird Watching
I've been watching the birds outside my
window for so long,
I've acquired the ability to read beaks.

Robin Williams

I wish I could send my books to

Robin Williams.

464

Life makes me nervous.

Roaches or people, which came first?

The only difference between an asshole and an asshole with money, is the amount of people the asshole with money can hurt.

No one really knows the pain others feel.

Beware of people who don't understand tongue in cheek.

Everyone you know is hiding something.

465

BY THE WAY, IF YOU'VE NEVER BEEN
"OVER THE TOP,"
YOU SHOULD TRY IT SOMETIME.

Even the pain that "never goes away,"

goes away.

Some men just don't
know how to be daddies.

Even a long life is a blink in time.

I now sit at home happily
because I traveled so much begrudgingly.

Different Journey
Different Scenery
Different Opinions

You can live in a lot of places
but you will only die in one,
unless you do Standup.

Tattoos

If you woke up with that shit growing on
you, you'd freak.

Mentally ill
or
mentally too aware?

"Artists are supposed to observe life."
Gregg Alexander- The New Radicals

While ignorance can lead to stupidity,
surprisingly it doesn't always begin there.

Although it's always nice to find someone who
agrees with me,
any open-minded thinker is like striking gold.

A Sixty to a Thirty in 2021

I'm twice as old as you but don't know
half as much as you.

Woke up one day without a care, turned on the
news and ended up in therapy
by the end of the day.

Being from New Orleans, I was always self
conscious about how I sounded,
until I experienced James Carville.

Would you rather be
ignored or criticized?

Why do we allow the stupid and greedy
to ruin things?

The most important lesson that should be taught
by parents is not how to make a living but rather
how to enjoy life while doing it.

If you are enjoying your alcoholism,
by all means, don't stop drinking.

I'm cursed with being a thinker, even worse,
a compassionate thinker,
deeply flawed but a thinker.

If you only do what you're told, your life
will be whatever you were told.

When you're not like everybody else,
you still have to make friends
with everybody else.

Evening News

I'm not sure what depresses me more,
the evening news
or the drug commercials during
the evening news.

The only thing I owe my family is a bill for
psychotherapy.

Evil is relentless.

When your children hit the hurting parts of
life, you know, reality, please remember,
they never asked for any of it.

If you need any more proof that racism is stupid, just look at the people they elect to represent them.

The truth is, I had the most fun when I made the least amount of money.

Most of you would've sat down and **stayed** seated if you would've been forced to walk in my shoes.

Assholes must be a necessary part of the ecosystem.

*"**We** tell people how to treat us."*
Richard Bryant

The size of the ego is not always equivalent to the size of the intellect.

He was moving like a New Orleans waiter, the snails kept speeding by.

I never got laid by being polite.

Homosexuality
If you don't teach kids that it's weird, then it's not weird.

The last thing I would want for my children is wealth.

HYSTERICAL WOMAN
The best way to describe me when I get angry.

You ever notice there are some people who
have everything it takes to be cute,
but they're not.

Hacked
All this convenience is causing a lot
of inconvenience.

Tech
**It's pretty obvious that you are courting
the Trojan horse.**

Don't you think we should've made the tech
companies fix hacking before we gave them
the keys to our very existence?

Everybody I've known has been
afraid of something.

473

If you dumb yourself down to make friends, your friends will most likely be dummies.

the honest horse player
"Today, the plan is to piss some money away and come home broke."

Life beat the idealism out of me before the age of 21.

Death, when everything that matters no longer does.

Fashion makes it about your looks, not your intellect.

While I don't believe that we're all born with the same intellectual potential, I do believe we all deserve an equal chance to find out.

Everyone is looking for a savior to forgive them for their ugly behavior.

"Search me" disappeared around the same time as "That's swell."

Men did not create their sexual drive.

Even though they can sometimes be a lot of trouble, there are times that I wished I'd had a vagina.

Leave it to Beaver

The internet has turned into Eddie Haskell on steroids.

Actually, most everything we do is an actually.

"You will experience the pain you inflict."

Dr James Kimmel

Money is only a tool and should not be
allowed to
make a tool out of you.

Ignorance is colorless.

Things don't always end up the way you
planned but they always end up.

I've never really felt comfortable
in adult skin
but I'm really good at being a kid.

Regulations help to stop
assholes from being
bigger assholes.

Are you preparing your children
for a world that no longer exists?

Had I been a girl, I would've changed the
way men treat women a long time ago.

A Pretty Long One Liner....

We met a guy in Portland OR
who told us that he had so much
THC coursing through his body
that the dogs at the airport
go crazy every time he goes
through a checkpoint.

Another pretty long one liner...

We have NO say in where we're born,
what color our skin will be,
how wealthy our parents are,
what religion we are
indoctrinated into
but we are judged by these facts
for the rest of our lives.

Yet another pretty long one liner...

Always remember,
Oz never actually did anything for
Dorothy and her three companions
except to point out to them that what
they were asking for was already
present in each of them
and that their journey was proof.

The Longest of the One Liners....

Anyone who has a billion dollars
either exploited a monopoly
that should've been broken up,
got inside information
unavailable to other investors,
bribed some politicians
or inherited the money from their
parents
(who did one of the above).

Robert Reich - former Secretary of Labor

Book V

Farewell to the Shell

Balls

I've sent copies of *"The Shell Books"*
to some of the best comics and writers
in America.
That takes balls.
And even though most of them didn't say
thank you,
it felt good to know that my thoughts
are possibly in the same room as theirs.

"The Shell Books"

Not once do I ask any of my readers to agree
with any of my thoughts and opinions.
READ, THINK and DISCUSS.
Those are my only requests.
I didn't even ask for money.
I don't want your money.
But I would like to know what you think.
But remember "The Curse."
Note: if you do agree with everything
I've written, you may want to seek
medical attention.
End of Note.

But hey

But hey, I did a lot of stuff in between.
This is what it turned out to be:

Some of the stuff was exciting.
Some of the stuff was funny.
Some of the stuff pissed me off.
Some of the stuff hurt me deeply.

But hey, I did a lot of stuff in between.
This is what it turned out to be.

Success

Don't ever be ashamed of your success.
I have made that mistake.
Remember, new friends only know
the successful you.
Leave the lesser you behind.
If old friends have a problem
with your success,
leave the lesser friends behind, too.

It was the Culture of the Times

I learned how to treat women from three men.

1. My father.

2. Hugh Hefner.

3. Sean Connery, "James Bond."

And don't forget the Playboy and James Bond
phenomenon was accepted in polite society.
Of course, I see things differently
as an old man.

Proceed with Caution
If something in "A Boomer Bible" upsets
you, best you stay away from these 4
comics' standup videos. Jim Jefferies,
Bill Burr, George Carlin and Bill Hicks.
Their take on politics, sex and religion
makes my writing seem tame.

Hand Me Downs

Rich people aren't necessarily good people. In fact, the majority of wealth is handed down to young people who haven't earned any of the wealth themselves. Many of the wealthy children that I've met were conditioned to feel entitled. I've heard rich fathers tell their sons that they are different from regular boys. That their families are different from regular families. One of the fathers who told his son this in front of me, was a dirtball. Like father, like son. The son became a dirtball, too. The father was a racist. Like father, like son. The son became a racist, too. He seemed like a decent rich kid until I got to know his father. Most, if not all, of their money was made off the backs of the poor. They despised poor people and called each race by their derogatory names.

I worked for these people. I made really good money. I have mixed feelings about that money because it also helped to enrich them. But ya gotta work somewhere. I was able to quit these guys but when I needed a job I had little choice but to work for people like them. It didn't matter the city. It didn't matter the job. A racist white guy usually owned the company.

This is America.

Aaron Rogers

Hey, young man, next time you step in shit, wipe it off. Don't wipe it all over yourself. Dr Joe Rogan? Are you kidding me? Really? So sad. I'm much older than you Aaron, seventy, and have seen the Joe Rogan's come and go. So sorry that you've decided to waste that Berkeley education.

When it affects the health of others you have no right to be a "free thinker." You have an obligation to be a decent human being. And I'm one of the most free thinkingest Motherfuckers you've never met. I'll share with you my opinion of people like Joe Rogan. I won't even waste an opinion. That's what I think of your "new friend." I hope you're embarrassed one day. The muscle bound steroid freak who makes his living by getting desperate people to do degrading and disgusting things for money (Fear Factor), (human cock fighting). Embarrassed? I meant ashamed.

Now I can say that I once told Aaron Rogers off. I won't but I could.

Abortion

The same people who attacked the Capital on January 6th in the name of freedom, would restrict a woman's freedom when deciding what to do with her own body.
How do you reason with that?
You don't.
You vote.
When a person wants freedom but only for themselves.
How do you reason with that?
You don't.
You vote.
You don't reason with it but you find a way to coexist and hope they do, too.
And you vote.
Right to Life? Capital punishment? War? Self defense? You've already made exceptions to the right to live.
So get off your "right to life" high horse and take care of the children that are already here.

T and A

I think it would be wise for women who want men to respect them for their minds, to have a talk with the women who flaunt their bodies in the workplace. I think the men of today (2022), are finally getting the point. But are the women of today getting the point? If you put your looks at the forefront, (hair, makeup, cleavage, leggings) or any other underwear, you may get noticed but your intellect will occupy the back seat. Change will not come by blaming men. If you want to be fair, start from within.

Man do I need a drink

Every civilization since the beginning of time has fermented fruit to make alcohol. If life is such a gift, answer one question. Why have humans fermented fruit to make alcohol since the beginning of time?
Please think hard before you have children.

The Opposite Sex

Women were to dance with.
Women were to have fun with.
Women were to be tender with.
Women were to be pleasured.
I never consciously thought of women as
sex objects.
However, there were many in my life
that wanted to be nothing else but.

Life is a lot different and God is great
when you live in a million dollar
beach house.

Avoidance

There are some folks whose opinions
we should not ignore.
We shouldn't ignore the opinions
we disagree with.
But we should try to avoid the people
who give them as often as possible.

70's Culture...

If I were a young man today, I feel confident that I'd not only treat women differently but life differently. I came of age in the 1970's. Today, Playboy Magazine would not play a prominent role in developing my psyche. I wouldn't know what Playboy was or who Hugh Hefner and James Bond were, (the Sean Connery, James Bond). How women were portrayed in movies and in print, was how women would be treated in neighborhoods, bars and businesses.

Back then, it was prestigious for a woman to be a Playboy Bunny or Playmate. Young women couldn't wait to put on a skimpy "Bunny" outfit and prance around. Men acted the way men act when women highlight certain body parts. And look, we don't even know why. Here's a concept; why not quit teasing us? And tell your friends. It's not fair to judge us if you don't tell your friends.

After I wrote this, I realized how hard it must be for young people today.

LOOK AT ME

LOOK AT ME, LOOK AT ME, LOOK AT ME, LOOK AT ME
LOOK AT ME, LOOK AT ME, LOOK AT ME, LOOK AT ME
LOOK AT ME, LOOK AT ME, LOOK AT ME, LOOK AT ME

PLEASE CONTINUE TO LOOK AT ME

LOOK AT ME LOOK AT ME LOOK AT ME LOOK AT ME
LOOK AT ME LOOK AT ME LOOK AT ME LOOK AT ME
LOOK AT ME LOOK AT ME LOOK AT ME LOOK AT ME

PLEASE CONTINUE TO LOOK AT ME

LOOK AT ME LOOK AT ME LOOK AT ME LOOK AT ME
LOOK AT ME LOOK AT ME LOOK AT ME LOOK AT ME
LOOK AT ME LOOK AT ME LOOK AT ME LOOK AT ME

PLEASE CONTINUE TO LOOK AT ME

LOOK AT ME LOOK AT ME LOOK AT ME LOOK AT ME
LOOK AT ME LOOK AT ME LOOK AT ME LOOK AT ME
LOOK AT ME LOOK AT ME LOOK AT ME LOOK AT ME

PLEASE CONTINUE TO LOOK AT ME

LOOK AT ME LOOK AT ME LOOK AT ME LOOK AT ME
LOOK AT ME LOOK AT ME LOOK AT ME LOOK AT ME
LOOK AT ME LOOK AT ME LOOK AT ME LOOK AT ME

PLEASE CONTINUE TO LOOK AT ME

LOOK AT ME LOOK AT ME LOOK AT ME LOOK AT ME
LOOK AT ME LOOK AT ME LOOK AT ME LOOK AT ME
LOOK AT ME LOOK AT ME LOOK AT ME LOOK AT ME

LOOK AT ME LOOKING AT ME

Those Seventeen Years

Certainly a minority child raised in a ghetto, by a single mother, experiences sights and sounds far more extreme than I experienced during the seventeen years I lived in my father's house.

Childhood trauma is childhood trauma. I used to feel guilty for feeling depressed. After all, there were no rapes and murders in the neighborhood I was raised in. No shots were ever fired in anger. No violence to speak of. I'm seventy and I still feel the pain of my father's alcoholism. Those seventeen years never went away.

Marrying

If your reason for marrying was one of the
following; you will divorce.
The only question is when.
Money
Looks
Sex
Social standing
Children
Social climbing

Boys to Men

In the world I was raised in, women were a
notch below anyone with a penis.
It was so accepted by society that I didn't
notice anything was wrong.
The women in my neighborhood not only
accepted it but embraced it.
I rarely heard a woman complain about her
lot in life unless the guy was a dirtball.
This indoctrination crossed the lines of race
and religion.
From an early age, no matter what race you
were, a boy was told that he was better than
a girl.
What do you mean you let a girl beat you?
If women expect to be treated differently,
they will have to start with the little boys.
We are only what you teach us.

I've lived in a house

I've lived in a house
where the faucets all dripped.
I've lived in a house
where everyone had flipped.
I've lived in a house
but didn't know what to do.
I've lived in a house
maybe so have you.
I've lived in a house
that had nothing much to say.
I've lived in a house
that said it anyway.
I've lived in a house
you know, I just couldn't stay.
I've lived in a house
seemed to be no other way.
I've lived in a house
I'm so grateful I got away.
I've lived in a house

The Truth about the "Burbs"

If you were raised in the suburbs, got
married and then moved back to the suburbs,
you are probably afraid. I believe suburbia is
a scar on all human existence. Suburb people
are always afraid. You have surrounded
yourself with the suburban mentality. It's a
form of mental inbreeding. If you moved to
the suburbs because you thought it was safer
than the city, why are you still afraid?
Because there's no diversity, that's why. All
you know is suburban life. Every
conversation is the same. That's one of the
reasons kids raised in the suburbs are angry.

The suburbs   are mostly superficial.
The suburbs   waste a lot of gas.
The suburbs   are pockets of racism.
The suburbs   breed followers not thinkers.
The suburbs   were not built by craftsmen.
The suburbs   are still segregated.
The suburbs   serve only the developer.
The suburbs   introduced the driving
              commute.
The suburbs   are one of the reasons for
              global warming.
The suburbs   were a mistake.

The "N" Word
Or
Richard's Lament

My hope is that one day different races can once again make fun of one another. Not in a mean way but the way my black friends and I could years ago. No one got offended. We'd go to BB King concerts together and get high and listen to Richard Pryor albums. The "N" word was just part of a regular conversation. None of my black friends were "niggers." It was just a word to us.

If you are close friends, you should be able to joke around. If you are real friends, you should be able to say anything. While I completely understand the pain that the word has caused, so did Richard Pryor. The answer, as usual, is somewhere in the middle. I don't use it 'cause all my black friends are dead. And I have never used the word in anger or in a derogatory way. To be clear, I feel that there is an appropriate way and place to use all words.

The Cheerleader Hypocrisy

Being a sports fan from the South, I noticed a great hypocrisy many years ago. The people who claim to be the most pious, the most in line with the teachings of the Bible, dress their girls and women in skimpy outfits and ask them to do writhing dance moves in front of thousands of jacked up men, every Saturday and Sunday in the fall.

They dress like sex objects but they're called, "Cheerleaders."

Responsibility Disclaimer

Please remember, not all of the pieces are about me or relate to me in any way. Similar to Randy Newman, I write some stories about people I've never met, places I've never been and subjects I think should be discussed.
Maybe they were silly.
I like silly.
Maybe the thought was poignant.
Poignant's OK.
Maybe in the third person.
There's way more than three.
Maybe about you, you probably noticed those.
Maybe the rhyme just worked.
Sometimes for me, the piece doesn't even have to make sense if the rhyme sounds nice.

Disciple Tryouts

Although I've never seen it written
about in any of the old texts, I've often
wondered, could there have been
tryouts for "Apostle," similar to
"The Bachelor?"
And if there were tryouts for Apostle,
were haircuts as important back then
as they are now?
Were there designer robes and jewelry?
Were the chariots they arrived in rented
just for the show?
Other than Judas, (that bastid), were
there any other backstabbers?
What was the criteria other than
total commitment?
Most people want to know something
about the authors of each
book of the Bible.
I want to know more about the editors.

Mein Fuhrer

To all the supporters of "d rump,"
please stop hiding behind this sentence,
"I like his policies."
His policies are bigotry and bullshit.
The next time you're asked why you support
this asshole,
just say,
"I'm a racist
and
I've been waiting for a leader
my whole life."

"God Games"

Are earthquakes and wildfires
planned in advance by God
or
are they just
"God Games"
that got a little out of control?

I'm Drinkin' Again

You know I cut my teeth
and I've paid my dues
and at seventy six,
I got nothin' to lose.

I'm drinkin' again.
Alone or with a friend.
I'm drinkin' again.

Most all my friends are gone
you heard what I said.
And when I lay down
It might be MY death bed.

So, I'm drinkin' again.
Alone or with a friend.
I'm drinkin' again.

Now don't be worried
or concerned,
'cause I plan on using
the lessons I've learned.

But I'm drinkin again.

Truth is, I don't care
what you think.
And I'm havin' more than one,
so gimme another drink.

'Cause I'm drinkin' again.
Alone or with a friend.
I'm drinkin' again.

You know I really don't care
how it turns out.
I realized a while back
you'll never figure it out.

So I'm drinkin' again.

I haven't been afraid of death
for many, many years.
And I didn't need therapy
to dissuade those fears.

'Cause, I'm drinkin' again.

Some Clooney tequila
and Johnny Walker Blue.
Whatever Dylan's sellin'
I'll have some, too.

'Cause I'm drinkin' again.
Alone or with a friend.
I'm drinkin' again.

I could write another verse
but that would be a sin.
'Cause I know how this ends up
even before I begin.

But I'm drinkin' again.
Alone or with a friend.
I'm drinkin' again.

Disclaimer: I'm only seventy so you have six
years before you have to worry. BUT I'M
DRINKIN' AGAIN!

The Meaning of Life

I was one sentence away from learning the
"meaning of life."
I had been sitting at a bar deep in the
French Quarter for many hours, listening to a
"French Quarter Shaman" pontificate.
We had been drinking heavily.
At the exact moment the Shaman started to
speak about the
"meaning of life,"
I was distracted by a guy telling a joke at the
table next to us. So I missed what the Shaman
had to say and the "meaning of life"
slipped away.
So did the "French Quarter Shaman."

A Job Interview 2022

Look, I don't come in early on Monday
mornings and I get off at noon on Fridays.
I'll give you 2 or 3 good days a week.
That's just the way it is.
Am I hired?
And by the way, when can I expect my
first check?

Child Rearing

Before you have children it might be wise to ask
yourself this question; who will raise them?
You or society? By the way, I know the answer.
It's society.
So prepare yourselves.

With the Innocence of an Adult

Your children's world will be nothing like
yours was.
And by the age of five, they will know more
than you ever will.

Genitalia

To be honest, I could've done without
genitals. Certainly, this design anyway. There
are some obvious changes I would make. First
of all, no more periods. Secondly, erections on
demand. I'm open to anything else but those
two are definites.

Future Food Consumption

The way humans eat will completely change in twenty years. Everyone won't be happy. A baby born today will probably never eat a sub or a po boy sandwich for lunch. A baby born today will not look at a steak dinner as something special but rather something foolish. Today is October 20, 2021, do you know what your baby will do for a living? I'm sorry, did I say baby? I meant person. We're only babies for a short period of time. Make sure you remember that before you procreate.

Differences

You must've breathed different air.
You must've met different people.
You must've experienced nature differently.
Your work is different.
You definitely had different parents.
You sound different.
You look different.
You think different.
Yes, we have our differences.

There are only Two

Each generation of Americans gets two
black celebrities.
That's the limit.
And right now it's Steve Harvey
and Michael Strahan.
I wish someone would ask them to
"just say no." There are other black men
who could use the work.

Are you Afraid?

Are you afraid that someone will find
out you're afraid?
Would you act tough
if you didn't feel like you had to?
You will only achieve tough
when you stop acting tough.

Got me Twisted

Breakin' up- got me twisted.
Loneliness- got me twisted.
Alcoholism- got me twisted.
Drugs- got me twisted.
Weekend comin'- got me twisted.
Weekend here- got me twisted.
Weekend over- got me twisted.
Nighttime falling- got me twisted.
Politicians- got me twisted.
Some friends- got me twisted.
Liars- got me twisted.
Yeah, I know what twisted is all
about.

Privilege
I don't know about you
but I deserve MY white privilege.
I'm white.
Believe me, there's absolutely
no other reason.

the men who hit on me

the men who hit on me wore suits
the men who hit on me wore uniforms
the men who hit on me were professionals
the men who hit on me were blue collar
the men who hit on me were holy
the men who hit on me were manly
the men who hit on me were academics
the men who hit on me were athletes
the men who hit on me were close friends
the men who hit on me were drunk
the men who hit on me were sober
the men who hit on me were all kinds of
people

the men who hit on me
While I'm not gay, you cannot convince me
that homosexuality is not as natural
as heterosexuality.
Especially, now that you've read
"the men who hit on me."

Talkin' 'bout my generation

Roberta and I have been watching a lot of
old black and white movies.
People haven't changed much
in a hundred years.
There's a percentage who hope;
there's a percentage who try;
then there's the overwhelming percentage
of those who just accept.
These percentages seem to
remain constant.
This generation has a chance to fix
what my generation didn't.
But it won't.
None do.

Where does the time go?

Everyday it gets sucked into a black hole
called the past.
Get too close to the rim and you could get
transported back to high school.

Heaven or Hell?

I consider my conscience to be my soul.
Therefore, I believe that when I die
my soul dies with me.
And ya know, you shouldn't get angry
if we disagree.
Think of it this way, I won't be around
to bother you in Heaven.

Difference between China and US

American kids are not in the mood.
Chinese kids do what they're told.

The System

Assholes are more than likely the
product of parents who either didn't
care or didn't know shit.
But we blame the assholes don't we,
when we should be blaming the
parents or maybe the system.

Mouthful

Let's try to stop this infestation
that's spreading all around the nation.
What we need is education
to improve this situation.
Just a fair interpretation
a totally honest explanation.
I hope you give consideration
to my simple variation
and pass the Goddamned legislation
to finally end discrimination.

The British

You ever notice how the guys who
invented the English language,
don't even use all the letters
of the alphabet?
Why even have an "H"
if you plan on riding a orse to ospital?

Aging

If you expect to be desired in your forties and
fifties, the way you were in your twenties, you
will more than likely be disappointed.
Respect is really what we should be looking for
as our body ages.
"He doesn't look at me, you know,
the way he used to."
Well, you don't look like you used to look.
This is just another one of life's gifts.
It's called aging. Erections don't just happen,
they have to be caused. And don't blame men
because unlike women we can't fake it. But you
do have two things that don't age, no, not your
breasts. The two things that don't age are
your smile and your intellect.

Tasteless

On more than one occasion I have been
tasteless.
Sometimes I was tasteless
because I was drunk.
Sometimes I was tasteless
because at times I'm tasteless.
Who knows why we do some of the things
we do.
Tasteless

No Place Left to Land

If you're under fifty years of age,
I'm not sure you'll understand
but this piece is about
having no place left to land.

I flew around for years
rarely thinking twice.
With so many places to land,
man it sure was nice.

All the airports were so friendly.
I was always welcomed in.
And even tho we weren't related,
I felt like next of kin.

The friends I used to turn to,
the places I used to go,
the universe is slowly taking,
everything I know.

It really doesn't matter
if you are a woman or a man.
If you live long enough,
you will come to understand.

The universe will leave you
with no place left to land.

More about titty meat

The more titty meat you show the less your intellect is noticed. If you are sexualizing your persona, don't be surprised if men think of sex when they see you.

no time for petty

no time for petty
too close to the end
no time for petty
don't let it begin
just stop yourself
you know that you can
'cause there's no time for petty
you're just too close to the end

To Dave Chappell,
While it's great to make fun of evil, it's not funny
to make fun of the innocent. Remember,
"blackface" wasn't a big problem in the
White community.
Hopefully, I'm alive to see the "I get it" tour.

512

Anything at all

If we need to talk, we'll talk.
If we need to dance, we'll dance.
If we need to dine, we'll dine.
If we need to drink, we'll drink.
If we need weed, we'll smoke it.
If we need to spend ALL the money,
we'll spend ALL the money.
Anything to get to the VAGINA, baby!
Anything at all!

Myself

I've embarrassed myself
I've amazed myself
I've hated myself
I've loved myself
I've entertained myself
I've shit myself
I've talked to myself
I've discovered myself

street kids

take your medicine
sit back down
keep your mouth shut
don't make a sound

when the boy spoke up
he got a lotta flak
so he left home
and he never came back

while you can guide a child
you can't tell 'em what to think
that boy left town
'cause he was on the brink

he had to learn the hard way
that they don't care what you think

so take your medicine
sit back down
keep your mouth shut
don't make a sound

Regular Guy

He was such a regular guy,
who married himself a regular wife.
Together they lived a regular life,
one without much stress or strife.

He tried to change
but he could not.
She seems OK
with what she's got.

He was such a regular guy.
His children were the regular kind.
The type of children
that are easy to find.

A boy and a girl
in that order, you see
and they knew exactly
what they wanted to be.

Yes,
he was such a regular guy.
Not the kind
that would catch your eye.

He tried to change
but he could not.
And she seems happy with
what she's got.

Pray Down/Pray Up

Pray down to the Devil.
Pray up to God.
Cry out in the night
it all seems so odd.
'Cause there's no one listening
in the sky or underground.
You're merely talking to yourself
just moving thoughts around.
But if it gives you peace
to think someone is listening,
hold on to those beliefs
you were given at the Christening.

Free-dumb of Religion

This is a real news headline from
2022:
"Toxic foam coats sacred river.
Hindu worshipers bathe in it."

Wildfire

My car burned up,
my house did, too.
We tried to put it out
but there wasn't much we could do.
Wildfire
You know, it happened last year
and the year before that, too.
And every year they say
the same thing.
There's nothing you can do.
Wildfire
This year was even worse,
had to run for our life.
We barely escaped,
me, my dog and my wife.
Wildfire
Why'd they let us build here?
Who said it was OK?
They knew it was a fire zone
(back then),
the proof showed up today.
Wildfire

Competition

I don't get too competitive.
It just seems so repetitive.
I always lose interest
either way.

I beat you.
Maybe you beat me.
As long as we both
feel victory.

You're on top.
Really, so what?
I'm really just happy
to have made the cut.

I don't get too competitive.
It just seems so repetitive.
I always lose interest
either way.

Especially when it happens
day to day.

Let it Go

Everybody seems:

defensive
or
hurt
or
flooded
or
burned out
or
burnt out
or
quaked
or
invaded
or
deserted
or
melted
or
just plain blown away!

Gotta Ring that Bell

No matter what religion it is that rings your
bell, you don't necessarily stop being friends
with folks whose bell is rung by a
different theology.
Why not give the same respect to an atheist?
After all, they're using something called
common sense.

The Good the Bad and the Ugly

I believe a parent's job is to expose children
to as much as possible.
The good, the bad and the ugly.
The ugly might matter the most.
Taking time to explain each.

Old Cajun

I asked the "Old Cajun" about work and money.
This is what he said;
"I'm mon told y'all somethin' 'bout
woik and money.
Po people woik,
rich people make da money."

"The Stupids"

I wonder who put "the stupids" in charge.
Seems their constituency
has grown pretty large.
Not much you can tell "the stupids,"
unless it's filled with hate.
'Cause that is a feeling that must be fulfilled
and "the stupids" can hardly wait.
It's so easy to rile up "the stupids."
The ringmaster need only appear.
No, it doesn't take much
to excite this bunch.
They just needed a purveyor of fear.

Diamond Girl

Although I foolishly purchased a diamond
ring for a woman many years ago,
I would never do it again.
I would not want to spend my life with
someone who thinks those overpriced rocks
have value. Wanting or needing a diamond
says so much about who you are
and what you value.

Old Cajun

I asked the "Old Cajun" what he thought
about love. He said,
"Ya know, you can neva get enuf love."
Then he said,
"dare was dis gurl, she was two years younga
dan me. She was beaudiful and very funny.
An Caw Damn, dat gurl was pretty.
In fact, she's still pretty.
She became your Gran Maw Maw.
And this "Old Cajun" could neva
get enuf a her.
Dat's what I think about love, Sha."

Religions

If you want to believe bizarre stories,
isn't it pure hypocrisy not to respect my right
to not believe bizarre stories?
And for those who are offended
by my thoughts and conclusions,
please remember, the world is being run
by people who also disagree with me.
What do you think about
the job they're doing?

3 stages of "Fame Worship"

1. Fame Enthusiast
2. Fame Junkie
3. Fame Whore

I think my friend has a monkey.
Seems she's become a fame junkie.
She can't get enough.
She always needs more.
Could it be she's become what we call a
"Fame Whore?"

The office of
Dr William "Will" Hertchabalz
& Dr William "Willy" Hertchabalz Jr
Urology

Excuse me, are you Dr Hertchabalz?
No I'm not,
I'm Dr "Willy" Hertchabalz Jr
Dads not in today.

Image and Likeness

I cried for my father the other day.
I actually felt the pain
that I imagine he felt during his life.
I was sitting in my chair
and I imagined his face in my
facial expression.
There was no mirror in the room.

Dogs, Words, Clothes

Certain clothes
say
Certain things
in
Certain places
Check out their dogs,
listen to their words
and see how they're dressed.
That's all you need to know.

Surfin' USA

I met a wise old surfer while walking on the beach one day. He was one of those soft spoken, gentle souls that when you cross paths with in life, you say to yourself, is this guy for real? I had met a guy like that years ago when living in Boulder, Colorado. The soft spoken gentle guy in Colorado turned out to be a phony; (fucked all the girls and stole all the money). So I take the words of a charismatic soft spoken seemingly gentle soul with some trepidation. Anyway, I asked the surfer if he had any advice for young surfers. This is what he told me,

"No matter how high the wave, or how great the ride, every wave has to return to the shoreline.
Remember, it's how you treat the people
that are waiting there that matters.
It's not what you accomplish,
it's how you act afterwards."

MMA and Fear Factor
Exploiting desperate people
doesn't make you a smart businessman.
It makes you a person
who exploits poor people for profit.

Flash Flood

We hoped and prayed
this time would be a dud.
But instead we were awakened
by large sticks and a lotta mud.

Flash Flood

It rained all night
real hard and windy, too.
There really wasn't much
that any of us could do.

Flash Flood

We weren't in a flood zone
before global warming
changed the terrain.
Seems that now there's a "Flash Flood"
every time there's a rain.

Flash Flood

We'll rebuild again
'cause that's what we always do.
But I felt obligated
to leave this letter for you.

Flash Flood

So we'll thank the Lord
that none of us were killed
and for the FEMA money
to help with the rebuild.

Flash Flood

Betrayal

It seems to happen
when you least expect it
and there's really
nothing that you can do

Betrayal

Because the person who you
loved and trusted
just stabbed you in the back
It's true

Betrayal

Is there a way to know
which way someone will go
when thick and thin get tested?

Betrayal

Your stomach churns
you might feel queasy
when betrayal is ingested
it doesn't go down easy

Betrayal

Is it Settled Law?

All the forced birthers
in Texas
appear to have have
gotten their way.
Causing the unwanted babies
to pay and pay and pay.
What about the girl
who'll be butchered and maimed.
None of these fanatics
even know her name.
I'm still hoping
for some intelligent debate.
But the folks with the intellects
keep showing up too late.
When I ask the next question,
it's sometimes met with laughter.
After you force the birth,
what about the after?

Murder he Wrote

I've never believed
that an abortion was murder.
But I've always believed
that shooting a doctor
who provides an abortion was.

Abortion Issue Again

There's a big difference between stepping
on acorns and chopping down trees. We
have many trees that need help and all you
want to talk about is the acorns. The
Republican Party uses the abortion issue
with the expertise of a brain surgeon. Why
else would poor people keep electing
people too rich to understand poorness?
I've believed for a long time that when a
woman decides to have an abortion,
she actually SAVES multiple lives.

They called him Kenny

I'm a fetus that should've been aborted.
I wasn't exactly what
the doctor had ordered.
The middle of three, "Oh boy, another life."
But that wasn't what my father said
to his wife. He'd slip up again
another five years down the road.
But by that time
his heart had grown cold.
Children are people.
They don't stay babies, you see.
You shouldn't have had one,
much less two and three.

Goo Goo Da Da

Having a baby
means having a teenager.
Having a baby
means having to deal with other parents.
Having a baby
is not for everyone.

Drip, Drip, Drip

Life goes rushing by unless you're alone
and depressed. In that case, you can hear
every second as it crawls past,
dragging with it whatever garbage
it picks up along the way,
stopping from time to time to wallow.

When you're alone

They say what defines you is the kind of
guy you are when no one is watching.
So obviously there are more jerk-offs
than previously thought.

Wall Street Titans Solomon, Gorman, Diamon

I know the beds you sleep in
are the best that money can buy.
I just read about the bonuses you're
getting and I can't help but wonder
why.
And although your beds are
expensive
and the price of your home is steep,
my question to all 3 of you
is
HOW THE FUCK DO YOU SLEEP?

"Klan Mom"
Thanks to Jimmy Kimmel

"The Stupids" have commandeered
the megaphone
and are making a loud
screeching sound
that is blocking out reason.

531

Toasters, Roasters, Coasters, Boasters and Ghosters

"The Shell Books" have put people into categories:

Toasters– Bravo, Ken!
Roasters– those who were deeply offended
Coasters– didn't see any meaning
Boasters– told me I was crazy
Ghosters– were never heard from again
"The Shell Books" showed me
who my friends and family really were.
This being the fifth and final book in the series,
I've dealt with some rejection and negativity.
Most of the negativity came from rich white
people, manly men and religious fanatics.
So I guess I did my job.
I still say that this has been the best feeling
I've had while writing.
If you don't show someone
who you really are,
you could be mistaken for someone else.

Epilogue to a Friendship

What about the friendships,
the ones that weren't real?
When all the time you were hoping
that they were the real deal.
Cloaked in artificial,
they now seem superficial.
I hope this makes it official.
Truth rising to the top.

The Evolution of Rap Music

(synthesized voice with some really nice music
playing in the background).
Bidda bidda bee
Bidda bidda baa
Bidda bee bidda ba
bidda bidda bee bidda bidda ba
I cut the bitch.
But don't hold me accountable
The obstacles I faced were almost
insurmountable.
She said no
when she shoulda said yes
So I cut the bitch...
Art?
Gil Scott-Heron must be turning over
in his grave.

Indoctrinated?

Most of us don't realize the level of
indoctrination that a human being
experiences from beginning to end.
Very few of your thoughts are original
and very few of your thoughts
are your own.
I know that probably hurts your feelings
but it's true.

Goatee

Since the beginning of time the goatee
belonged to artists and thinkers.
But now, it's been hijacked by middle
aged, conservative, white men.
What's up with that?
They must've found out
what the artists knew all along.
The girls just love 'em.

Discomfort

Seems some of the subject matter in
"The Shell Books"
has caused a little consternation.
I'm not sure exactly why.
I never ask anyone to believe
what I believe.
But I guess some of the pieces
make too much sense.
Some readers have responded with what I
consider self-righteous indignation.
I know, I know, you think I'm attacking
your mother. I'm not.
The books are meant to be discussed, not
burned. But once you're indoctrinated
it's almost impossible to break free.
I know a lot of you are walking around
feeling that what you believe is what
everyone should believe.
I feel sorry for your children.
Maybe you'll find that being opposed to
science and fact is not something that will
be of help to them later in life.

The Inheritor

He did nothing to deserve
anything great.
All he really did was
be born and wait.

The Inheritor

He hid behind quiet and cool.
Saying little or nothing
had become his rule.
And he certainly would be
nobody's fool.

The Inheritor

Recently forced to face
an unpleasant truth.
The final blow
from an unhappy youth.
All he wanted
was the proof.

The Inheritor

The proof is in the pudding.
The pudding is the dough.
The amount of the gift
was all he wanted to know.

The Inheritor

He did nothing to deserve
anything great.
All he really did was
be born and wait.

The Inheritor

Dress for Success

ACCEPTABLE- clean and comfortable.

PROFESSIONAL- maybe a little uncomfortable but definitely doesn't highlight any particular body part.

SEXY- highlights certain body parts and definitely NOT suitable for the workplace.

I am not a prude; sexy is actually my favorite.
But not at work,
unless you're a stripper or a hooker.

Green Socks

I have a friend who told me that he doesn't pray any longer and it's actually made his life better. He told me that now he depends on "green socks." He says that when he doesn't wear the "green socks," he feels naked and alone. But when he wears the "green socks" proudly, and lets as many people as he can see them, his life seems to be more positive and pleasant. I told him to keep wearing the "green socks."

It's not all Good
I rail against calling life a gift because
it's not a gift.
Let me ask you this;
is it a gift if you're born to starve to death?
Somalia? Bangladesh? Yemen?...
No, that's not a gift.
That's an atrocity.
The same people who say life is a gift,
are the same people who use the term,
"It's all good."
And no, it's not all good.

Push-up Bra
Women, we know you have breasts.
Why do you continue to highlight your liabilities?
Your tits will sag but your intellect
doesn't have to.

Exposed

I decided to send
"The Shell Books"
to
"old friends"
in order to find out if they were
"old friends"
or just old people I knew long ago.

Migrant

I'm sure glad I'm not a migrant.
They seem to be treated like shit.
I'm sure glad I'm not a migrant.
My personality just wouldn't fit.
They left home because they had to.
The reasons, more than a few.
It'd be nice if people understood,
there was nothing else that they could do.
I'm sure glad I'm not a migrant.
It's a hard life, that's what they say.
I bet a lot of them wouldn't be migrants,
if they could find happiness
and safety any other way.

Fried Liver

I can remember a conversation I had
with my liver when I was still drinking.
"Hey man, take it easy,
I gotta filter all that shit."
My response was the same every time.
"Hang in there bro, you'll make it."
My liver took a beating.

You're Out!

In 2021, a person at home
can umpire a baseball game better than
an actual umpire.
The same goes for referees
in football games.
The cameras are far more reliable.
So WTF?

What's worse?

What's better?

1. being a guy who sleeps with many
women and doesn't get married?

Or

2. being a guy who leaves his wife after
thirty years of marriage to sleep with
other women?
The answer is neither.
It's just a matter of personal choice.

The Women Believers

I've wondered for a long time how a woman could belong to any religion. All of the mythologies put the men in charge. The Apostles were all men. Why was that? Most of the stories relegate women to a position lower than that of a man. And you follow. Do you even know what your religion is all about? Do you know what it teaches? I think I'd find a way to live a full and happy life without the need to belong to a religion that makes me less than.

Praise the Lord

You say it because your momma did.
It gives you comfort.
That's all you know.
And although I understand why you
"Praise the Lord,"
it doesn't mean that the particular "Lord"
you're praising exists anywhere but in your
head. But Praise the Lord. Although I agree
with freedom of religion, I also agree with
freedom from religion.

Ten Men

I knew a woman who lived with
ten men.
She'd tell me about them all,
again and again.
She said she only married one
but ended up with ten.
And the ten she ended up with
she'd stay with till the end.
Then she told me she was glad
that they, too, decided to stay.
She said each one is special
in his own little way.
She told me that sometimes
each man would come and go.
She said she didn't know why
and she didn't have to know.
She said sometimes it gets hectic
if they all come over at once.
Ya know, 9 out of 10 ain't bad
'cause one of them is nuts.

10 Men (the alternate version)

One so funny it hurts from time to time.
One so clever he makes most everything rhyme.
One so happy his joy is hard to comprehend.
One so sad everyday seems like it's the end.
One so giving there's nothing left to give.
One so vicious his words cut like a convict's shiv.
One so strong nothing gets in his way.
One so timid he has nothing much to say.
One so weak he might not make it through the day.
One so loving I hope he never goes away.

Clock Time

My goal was never to be wealthy but rather to get to a point where I didn't have to pay attention to "clock time." After all, it's made up. It's not real. It might be midnight, it might be 1, 2, or 3 but I'm happy to say it doesn't matter to me.
I've made it past "clock time."

The Figments

The figments, they keep coming,
keep running to and fro.
The figments think they're real
but they're not and soon you'll know.
The figments enter slowly
bringing thoughts that aren't real.
Best be careful 'round the figments
cause your peace of mind they'll steal.

The Corcoran

While living in Washington, DC, I was a guest
of a member of the Corcoran Museum.
I may have attended two openings.
I forget what we saw.
But I clearly remember entering the museum.
I remember hearing a woman's voice saying,
"Something ought to be done."
We were stepping over homeless people
warming themselves on the grates
outside the museum.
I wondered if she meant let's fix the problem or
could somebody please get these dirty
Motherfuckers out of here.
Sadly, I think it was the latter.

VOTE and bring a friend!

How did we become the Left and the Right?
Who decided to draw the lines and fight?
Why'd we let them label our friends?
Who decides when this bullshit ends?
When will we realize that hate is a choice?
How do we get them to hear our voice?
VOTE and bring a friend!

Training Wheels

We've all cut someone off in traffic.
We've all made that big mistake.
We've all said the wrong thing in public.
We've all done the wrong thing at work.
We've all arrived too early.
We've all gotten there too late.
We've all cut someone off in traffic.
We've all made that big mistake.
But how many take time to acknowledge
that truly, we are all alike.
Except for what we learn
from our parents,
while learning to ride a bike.

Nursing Home

Stockpiled, waiting for this
"gift" to end.
Found myself sitting
in the return bin.
Old folks broken down,
never gonna mend.
Waiting for the final chapter
of life to end.
Not everyone achieves
this goal, you know.
The one where it's time
to get old and go.
All the pills we take
as a crutch.
The weekend visits
that mean so much.
The "gift" of life
is coming to a close.
Next week's bouquet
will be missing one rose.

When I lived in Vegas, I sold meat.
Mostly ham steaks and hot dogs for
a company called
"First Quality Sausage." Although most of my
sales calls were to casinos, I also called on
the chefs at Nursing Homes.
Sometimes I had to wait.

Most People

Most people will never visit the Grand Canyon.
Most people believe what they're told.
Most people don't get a chance to grow old.
Most people follow the crowd.
Most people are rarely loud.
Most people stick with their kind.
Most people never make up their mind.
Most people go to work everyday.
Most people have nothing to say.
Most people come home and complain.
Most people you meet won't remember your name.
Most people will never leave their neighborhoods.
Most people don't do much with their life, other than have two kids and a wife.
Most people

Scenery

Parents- what kind?
Education- how much?
Hometown- where?
Generation- how old?
Sex- which?
That's your scenery.

A Box of "Fuck You's"

Got a package
I wanna send,
to an enemy,
not a friend.
I wanna give 'em something
that I'm sure they can use.
So I'm sending them
a box of "Fuck You's."
A box of twelve,
maybe even twenty four.
And if they keep on acting up
I'll be glad to send some more.

Pain and being a "Real Man"

I'm glad that we're finally realizing that it's
mostly DNA. People who have high pain
thresholds are not better than people with
low pain thresholds.
But it's easier to be a bully isn't it?

Old

When there's nobody
left to tell
and the future is either
Heaven or Hell.

Old
When you're in
the room alone
and there's no one
left to phone.

Old
You've lived
a long life
Even outlived
your wife.

Old
When there's nothing
left to do
and the future's
not up to you.

Old

Death of a Grandpa

Embrace the change
don't fear it.
It's just the final part
of life.
In fact, it seems
you're running late
if you want to
catch your wife.

And a Firm Handshake

I started being rude to car salesmen after I
encountered my first one.
I've never cared for transactional
"friendships."
You know, the Capitalism kind.
That phony upbeat handshake.
That phony upbeat smile...

The Confrontational Bullshit of Life

Even the people who aren't considered prejudiced seem to be prejudiced against wimps. Yeah, that's true. And it seems to be ok. But just like skin color and hair color our personalities start with our DNA. And yet we call people names. And we feel superior. And to think, it's mostly just DNA and circumstance. So stop it. Stop calling people names and call out your friends when they do. I've always hated the confrontational bullshit of life. There was a time when I joined in and then came the time many years ago when I refused to participate.

Not Guilty?
I've seen so much in my life.
I just didn't think in a million years
that I would see a policeman,
who knew he was being filmed,
commit murder and then plead
"Not Guilty."
He was convicted.

Sunrise Services

Sunrise services 6 am
Sunday morning on Bourbon Street,
1973

Fuck you.
No, Fuck you.
Oh really?
Fuck you.
Roll in the streets, police come,
off to jail.

Sunrise services 6 am
Sunday morning on Bourbon Street,
2022

Fuck you.
No, Fuck you.
Oh really?
Fuck you.
Load pistol.
Shoot.
Police come, EMT's come,
coroner comes,
off to morgue.

Thanks for the Check

The only time you should care
about the Kardashians is when you get a
check from one of them in the mail.
Kourtney,
Hope it all works out. Thanks for the
check.
Hi Kim,
Got the check. Hope it all works out.
Thanks.
Khloe,
Hope it all works out. Thanks for the
check.

Memo to Founders

I think it would've been a better idea
to have NO slavery and
freedom FROM religion
in the Constitution.
Also, I hope the decision on the second
amendment on guns hasn't been finalized.
I think we should stipulate "muskets."
I just came from a school board meeting.

We Fight

There are some things
that come to light,
when every day
and every night,
We Fight.

The volume rises
my temperature goes up.
It takes a while
before we make-up.
We Fight.

We think we'll stop.
We hope that we might.
It's usually about
something petty or trite.
But We Fight.

We both must feel
that's it's our right
'cause it seems
that every night,
We Fight.

It really doesn't matter
who's wrong or who's right.
It might just be our way
of making love.
'Cause every night,
We Fight.

Wealth

What is it good for?
Absolutely nothing.
Say it again.
Wealth.
What is it good for?
Absolutely nothing.
Please keep your financial status to
yourself.

NFL Cheerleaders

Make you proud?
or
Make you cringe?

These women are not forced to wear
skimpy outfits that push their breasts
together nor is anyone holding a gun to
their heads when they bend over and point
their half naked asses toward the crowd.
Does anyone else see the hypocrisy?
Me too?

Middle Age

She was cute and twenty three
when they met.
Now she's fat and forty seven
and he wants a new corvette.

Middle Age
Has hit like a bomb.
Middle Age
Now THEIR daughter is a mom.

Middle age
Seems all the kids are grown
having babies of their own.

Middle age
Now divorce is on the table.
It's the end of this love fable.

Middle Age

God Comes Down,
Offers you a Deal

Your children will suffer heinous
atrocities during their lifetime but in
return be given eternal life.
As a parent, what would you think of
this proposition? Would you say, OK God,
give my daughter the business.
The whole shebang.
The worst of human experiences.

She'll be carjacked at twenty with a
baby in the back seat. God's will.

She'll become an alcoholic and
a drug addict. God's will.

She'll be kidnapped and tortured, raped
and left to die on the side of the road.
All part of God's plan.

But remember there's that offer of
Eternal Life in Heaven, surrounded by
other "right to lifers" but only if she
suffers here on Earth.
As long as she's assured eternal life,
it really doesn't matter how bad it is
while she's alive.

That's kinda what faith means to me.
And I want none of it.

God has a plan for all of us!

I just watched a plane crash into a
neighborhood killing an unsuspecting
UPS driver instantly.
This immediately made me think of an
all loving, all powerful God.
What about you?

RESPECT

Women were to be protected and respected.
That's how men my age were raised.
But here's what I learned.
Women deserve no more respect than men do.
Whether a person's genitalia
is on the inside or out,
should hold no importance
when considering
respect for another human being.

My Mind Apologizes to Me

Dear Ken,

I'm sorry I make you see so much.
I'm not sure why I do it.
It sure would make life easier
If I could just say, screw it.
Remember how long I've worked for
you and trust me, you know you can.
A mind is a terrible thing to waste.
I hope you'll understand.
That I'm the kind that rarely stops,
even when asleep.
I think it has a lot to do with
the company that you keep.

My Role Models

I've written about being role modeled by James Bond and Hugh Hefner. Remember, when I was coming of age, Playboy was highly respected. Women dressed in bunny suits and were treated like pets. During this time in my life, I never heard one woman complain about this setup. In fact, just the opposite. Many young women waited in line hoping to work at a Playboy Club. Where were the mothers of the "me too" movement? Boys learn what they're taught. It's so easy to criticize old men. But we all become our generation.

You will too.

"B" who you want to "B"

I've established myself as:

- a "B" team writer
- a "B" team poet
- a "B" team humorist
- a "B" team traveler
- a "B" team atheist
- a "B" team lover

I decided to be the best of the "B" team.

The Purists

Pure Capitalism will eat itself.
I know this statement is true.
It's been happening for over fifty years.
But ya know, eventually skid row came back.
All the homeless had to pack,
they bought 'em a ticket,
told 'em not to come back.
Yeah, they moved 'em out of town
and for a while,
there were no homeless around.
Problem solved.
Until all the homeless came back,
with different names.

Leggings for Men

I'm a seventy year old man and
I've recently decided to start wearing
leggings out in public.
No underwear, just leggings.
Is that ok?
If not, why not?

The Destroyer in Chief

Remember when we were all laughing
as d rump destroyed everything
that was important and sacred to us?
I was guilty, too at first.
But at least I stopped laughing
after the second debate.

Got Hypocrisy?

Arnold Schwarzegger was just on
Jimmy Kimmel cutting it up.
If my memory serves me right,
this guy cheated on his wife
with his maid,
who was also married at the time,
fathered a child and tried to keep it a
secret. Now he's given applause
on late night tv.

Suppertime in Sonora

The bobcats eat the bunnies.
The coyotes eat the cats.
A hawk swooped down
to snatch up a mouse.
A rattlesnake just swallowed a rat.
A roadrunner just showed up,
sniffin' around.
They eat the ones that
live underground.
It's suppertime in the desert
for everything that's wild.
And if you're an adult anything
you'd best protect your child.

Toxic

You need a gun to feel safe.
You need a beer to get laid.
You need money to feel successful.
You need power to feel comfortable.
But you need to lie about your feelings.
Yes, I guess you're a man.
All that pain and he never complained.
He was taught to lie about his feelings,
so he did.

It won't do any good

I'm close to the end of caring.
I don't even care what I'm wearing.
I don't care what you think.
I actually hope that I stink.

I'm close to the end of caring.

I'm not gonna shave anymore.
I'm not gonna drive.
No, I'm not glad I'm alive.

I'm close to the end of caring.

And what you might say
has no bearing.
I've made my decision.
No chance for revision.

I'm close to the end of caring.

Cock Fighting

MMA is not a sport.
It's cock fighting.
You can call it a sport but it's cock
fighting.
And we don't even let chickens do it
(legally). Educated people who watch
MMA have said the draw is that it's the
ultimate mono a mono.
No it isn't, it's desperation and
exploitation.
And it's dehumanizing.
Maybe you could stuff MMA fighter
heads and put them on a wall like:
deer heads
and bear heads
and moose heads
and leopard heads
and lion heads.
Fierce fighters all.
Now ask yourself one question.
Would you want your child to do it?
If the answer is yes, I'm wondering how
the Fuck you got my book and why are
you still reading it?

Highlites

If you highlite your shoes,
I will notice your shoes
and tell you how nice they look.

If you highlite your jewelry,
I will notice your jewelry
and tell you how nice it looks.

If you highlite your makeup,
I will notice your makeup
and tell you how nice you look.

If you highlite your breasts,
I will notice your breasts
and tell you how nice they look.
(and I might ask if they're real).

If you highlite your hair
I will notice your hair
and tell you how nice it looks.

If you highlite your ass,
I will notice your ass
and tell you how nice it looks.

If you highlite your intellect,
I will notice your intellect
and keep MY mouth shut.

That's it

For many years I've believed
that my conscience is my soul.
To me that means that when I die,
my conscience (ie. soul), dies with me.
It doesn't go anywhere.
Up or down.
Done.
Like me, it's dead and gone.

Black Friend

How many times have I heard the words,
"I'm not a racist; I have a black friend?"
The same amount of times
that I've said to myself,
"No, having a black friend
doesn't mean you're not a racist.
You may just be a racist with a black friend."

If the Sugar Goes Bad

It was getting much harder
to be happy and glad.
But it gets even worse
if the sugar goes bad.
Turn on the tv,
live war thanks to Vlad.
But it gets even worse
if the sugar goes bad.
COVID-19 just won't go away.
You'll need another booster,
that's what they say.
To the growing list of heartaches,
this too we must add.
But it gets even worse
if the sugar goes bad.
The sugar I speak of
comes not in a can.
It's the sweetness of love
between a woman and a man.
All of life's heartaches
are easier to take.
But you'd better choose wisely.
'Cause make no mistake,
it gets even worse,
If the sugar goes bad.

Brothers

Not always friends,
no, they don't always agree
but brothers for life
they'll always be.

Polite Society

At various times throughout history,
"polite society"
has accepted these seven traditions:

1. Slavery- "they're mine."
2. Class differences- "it's not your place."
3. Misogyny- "she's just a girl."
4. Stealing land from the indigenous-
   "savages."
5. Bigotry- "I don't like their kind."
6. Hazing- "stick your nose in shit, boy."
7. Segregation- "they have their own."

Best beware of "polite society."

My Friends

My friends are bigots.
My friends are racists.
My friends are misogynists.
My friends are poorly educated.
My friends are religious.
My friends are angry.
My friends are no longer my friends.

Creation

When life got unbearable,
humans created God.
I used the God mythology, myself.
I used the one that the people around me
were using.
I understand how and why it worked.
It's the psychology in the theology
that makes us feel better.

"MIDDLE CHILD" MOURNING

"MIDDLE CHILD,"
IS MY MEMORIAL, MY HEADSTONE.
IF YOU'VE RECEIVED A COPY AND WILL
MISS ME WHEN I DIE, YOU'LL BE ABLE TO
GRIEVE WITHOUT LEAVING THE COMFORT
OF YOUR OWN HOME.
PLEASE FIND A WARM SPOT TO KEEP IT.
I HATE THE COLD.

Ya know, I've been a lot of things.
But I've been a lot of other things, too.

NO
Ya know, Ken, we've been looking
at your beliefs.
And we think some of them are fine.
But there are a few of them
that we don't care for.
We'd like you to keep those to yourself, ok?

I go back and forth between sanity
and insanity. Sometimes I forget
which one I'm on.

Your children will not be living in the world
you want for them.
So why are you preparing them for that?

Being brilliant doesn't necessarily mean
you're smart. Being kind does that.

Avoidance is a way of life for some.
I try to avoid the avoiders.

Some people want children
for the wrong reasons.
What are yours?

Most people only have a few memorable
moments in their lifetime.
There were times when I had five in a week.

When I was young I thought everything
would feel better than it actually did.
With one exception.

High-tech is what the big boat raffle
at the mall used to be.
Do you know anyone who
ever won the boat?

Simple Math

Go forth and multiply.
But make sure you can add first.

I heard recently that it's normal
for all "good" parents to lie
to their children.
It's the great ones who don't.

I was so mad, I couldn't get the whole curse word out. You moth, you bas, why you coc.

Don't expect people to keep secrets.
Why do you have secrets anyway?

They say all you gotta do is try.
That's not true.
It also helps to be lucky.

Who are you and how did you get in here?
I'm a locksmith and I'm a locksmith.
Leslie Neilson, Police Squad

3 words that are used as proof
of a college education:
Moreover,
Furthermore and
Parenthetically.

Sliced bread was once the size of a
man's hand.
In 2020 it's the size of a dog's paw.

When I was young, women sat with their
legs closed. I'm not passing judgment,
just sayin'.

I'm really not sure why I know the things
I know.
I do not remember paying attention.

Similar to our immune systems,
our intellects,
when working properly,
kick in,
to control and defeat our emotions.
Hopefully.

575

Most people don't figure it out.
They're the lucky ones.

An atheist is really no different than
somebody who believes in a different faith.
An atheist has faith in science.

A winner can die a loser
and
a loser can die a winner.
But they both die.

I'm so glad my wife is an asshole
on occasion.
I couldn't live with myself if she wasn't.

If you never leave your neighborhood, your
beliefs will replay on a
continuous loop.
So although the information that caused
your beliefs has been updated,
you haven't been.

I don't get paid for writing any of this.
That makes it even more important.

Saying Thank You

You should never respond to kindness with
indifference.
You may need a friend one day.

It's pretty obvious I didn't create the
vagina or the reason for its existence, nor
did I have anything to do with the
engineering of the penis.
All I did was follow "The Science."

577

America just may be
the greatest country ever.
We've learned to make celebrities
out of garbage.

You asked for my thoughts and
prayers.
I thought you were asking for my
thoughts ON prayers!

"WHEN YOU'RE GETTING ROBBED,

YOU ONLY HAVE ONE JOB.

GET ROBBED!"

BOMANI JONES

Even perfect people die.
How perfect.

The Classics

Have you read The Classics?
When I think of The Classics,
I think of all the writing
that didn't get published.

I'm pretty sure that peanut allergies
didn't exist when I was young.
Similar to depression, it just didn't exist.

It's the stuff that supposedly matters
that actually doesn't.
Example: sports.

Believe Women?
All of them? Every last Fucking one of them?
What about the psychos?

Comedian Bill Burr

People who say,
"Get the Hell out of here,"
are usually over fifty.
People who say,
"Get the Fuck out of here,"
are usually under fifty.
The teenagers just pull out guns.

Other than the ones that feed us,
there are two miracle plants.
Aloe and Marijuana

I've gone through the
pre-cool years,
the cool years and
the post cool years.
So put some clothes on and
get off my lawn.

Dying

When you're lying on your deathbed
be sure to tell the truth.
You're about to be transported
to the place that's got the proof.

New Product
hits shelves today:
"GIULIANI JUICE"
Hair color for men.

Don't be a Snob

I'd like to point out one thing to all of
the academic elitists with
big name publishers.
Jim Morrison self-published.

There's something rotten in Denmark.
I think I just figured out what it is.

There was a time when you could
get my dander up.
But not anymore.
I had it all taken out when I had
my craw removed.

She won't look like that in twenty years
(maybe ten).
Do you love her or her looks?

There is no man upstairs.
There is no woman upstairs.
There is no upstairs.

Oh, Baby!
I've been on a thinking and writing binge.
It's the best feeling you can have
where an erection isn't involved.

These books are proudly
made in America
by descendants of immigrants.
(as is most everything else).

I recently heard that NFL commissioner,
Roger Goodell, made $128 million over the
last two years.
And that's ok in America.

He's a Nobody?
You should always treat a
nobody like a **somebody**.
Know why?
Maybe **somebody** will tell you one day.

And now, some One Liners or a little more Edgy Mark Twain

"Better to sleep with a sober cannibal than a drunk Christian."

Herman Mellville from Moby Dick

If we can't teach
"Critical Race Theory,"
is it OK if we teach
"Critical Race Fact?"

Over the years I've learned to

tolerate the rich

but it's been a struggle.

Sometimes I feel like a good person
trapped inside a
not so good person's body.

Do you go to church to learn how to
love your fellow man or do you go
to church to feel superior to your
fellow man?

Two people have sex,

fifteen years later,

YOU'VE got responsibilities.

When it comes to electing women
to public office,
their heart matters much more
than their vagina.

I'm always amused when I see a woman
dressed as a sex object,
complain about being treated like
a sex object.

One of my biggest disagreements with
Capitalism,
is that it measures success by
"how much" and not by "how."

My soul told me years ago
that he was willing to take
some chances.

I'm actually glad that I don't have some
of the college educations
that I've been around.

The d rump Presidential LIE-brary

It's scary to think of how many people believe things that aren't true.

Humanity

Humanity is going to end up with so many conveniences but very little humanity.

The results of your endeavor are never totally up to you, never.

A truly successful capitalist dies with the most money.

Famous people should never forget it's the unfamous that made you famous.

I just received a Happy Birthday card from the Pain Institute.

I get along well with most animals but I gotta be honest, I do have trouble with the sheep from time to time.

Dear Dave Chappell,

Any jokes about a minority that you're not, aren't funny.

"The Indica Hour"
4 pm ish

By the time I truly understood life,
It was too late to do anything about it.

I grieve for the grievers.

What we didn't realize for years,
was that the polloi was polloiing at
our expense.

We shouldn't have to be represented by
the rich.

On one level, I'm a very weak person and
yet I've accomplished quite a lot.

I've found that the happiest people don't pay attention.

I'm a retired Rabble Rouser.

SUCCESS IS PERSONAL

MAYBE IF I WOULD'VE HAD A DIFFERENT LIFE,
I WOULD'VE HAD DIFFERENT OPINIONS.

Junior
My ego is so big... I'm naming you after me.

Seems the uneducated are thinking too much.

If you've never been abused, you can't possibly
relate to those who have been abused.

Every generation has a Fucking
war story.

Freedom for all
or
freedom for all who agree with
(look like) you?

Nature made women sex objects, not men.

Did Mother Theresa have a dark side?

You won't know who your real friends
are until you get sober.

Love is truth delivered gently.

Like gravity, my mouth is
a double-edged sword.

COVID-19 is culling the herd of the
unvaccinated.

I don't necessarily
rail against religion,
I rail against hypocrisy.

**If you give everyone guns,
someone is gonna get shot.**

The only thing that really matters
is what's in front of you.

There's a whole new generation that
won't care what you think or fix
anything that was wrong
with the previous generation.

Qualms; I've had a few.

Are humans the invasive species?

The moment a big man makes
a little man feel big,
is the moment the big man becomes truly big.

Make the best of the first time,
it will only happen once.

I just realized that Pink Floyd's,
"Us and Them,"
was way ahead of the whole
transgender movement.

Lets see, physics and science

or

religion and hysteria?

The only people who really matter
are the people who like you.

UFO'S
How many times do they have to tell us,
"we don't know what it is?"

I'm pretty sure I've never been
"Steadfast."

Sexual reproduction is actually
Nature's Ponzi scheme.

I'm not afraid of death but
I'm deathly afraid.

If the Supreme Court takes up obscenity
again, the salaries for college football
coaches will have to be part
of the discussion.

If life doesn't break your heart,
maybe you haven't got one!

I don't get appalled, I go straight to pissed.

People have been beat up so much by life
that you can't even retaliate for bad behavior
and feel good about it.

The really smart kids can't be trained.

While I understand on some level
the need for religions,
I also see the need
to call BS when bullshit
is being spewed.

The Bible
A book that can be used to teach anything
that the speaker decides to teach,
whether it's true or not.

I've always respected people who

respected themselves

and did not boast about it.

My wife, perfect imperfection!

There are really only 3 words that get me in trouble. The three I shouldn't have said or the three I should've said.

Don't forget to teach your children about nuance.

It's the stupid ones who tell you how smart they are.

Negativity and Rejection usually become my inspiration.

Tradition
Lies that are told from generation to generation, usually having racist overtones.

The toilet paper shortage of 2020
There's a time when wealth doesn't matter.

One day I realized the only thing that separates us from farm animals IS sensitivity.

"I need ammunition, not a ride."

V Zelinsky, President of Ukraine

It will take generations to overcome the damage done by d rump.

Breaking News
Queen Elizabeth wipes her own butt
and admits that she could've been
doing it all along.

TRANSGENDER
SOMETHING FOR THE NEXT GENERATION TO
FIGURE OUT.

If pain glowed, I wouldn't have to whine.

Banned books are the best books.

On more than one occasion,
I've mistaken rich and privileged
for smart and kind.

As I get closer to my last breath,
the thing that I'll remember most
was just how much hypocrisy there was
during my lifetime.

Circumstance is as important as DNA.

Art Linkletter was an illegal.

Not one story in the Bible

is told by a woman.

Are clothes more important
than what they cover?

Most folks can't be who they really are.

Do you even realize it when you don't give a Fuck.

Almost every great American was also an asshole.

Let's be honest, leggings are not for everyone.

Most rich kids don't understand real friendship.

Charisma in use, please act with caution.

I've spent seventy years on Earth and haven't once depended on your opinion.

Time just can't keep a secret.

Wishing you had different relatives is just part of being human.

Oh, how I long for a mundane conversation.

If someone asks you what you're writing, the best answer is, "more and better."

It seems like the only goal of human existence is to make it easier.

603

My youth was plagued by
Catholicism.

Conservatives
That's what we call racists in America.

Why does there always seem to be
one piece missing in life?

When given a choice,
I always choose less pain.

Don't look to your friends to show you
who you are, your enemies will show you.

Why did an all powerful,
all knowing, God create stink?

Sometimes the children you think are
failing are really the
smartest kids in the class.

When you pay homage,
don't expect any change.

If some of my thoughts seem foreign to you,
it might be because you're just not used to
hearing the unvarnished truth.

If you don't use the power you have,
do you really have it?

I've always respected strong women
but rarely had sex with any of them.

Modern is temporary.

Feeling superior is proof positive
that you're not.

Privilege doesn't mean you're better,
only luckier.

A room full of phony,
we've all been in one.

America was started by
white supremacists with some good ideas.

606

All happy and successful people
aren't necessarily competitive.

How do civil engineers show anger?

The greatest country in the world
will not be the one that
allows everyone to carry a gun.

There comes a time in life when
everything was fifteen years ago.

If we tell the next generation the same lies
we were told, when reality hits, they too, can
become alcoholics and junkies.

My goal has never been to become famous but rather to be treated with the same respect as a famous person.

I would've liked to have gotten to know an elephant.

Kindness is genderless.

Now deceased comedian Bill Hicks shared his feelings on abortion:
"Why not love the people who are already here?"

A lot of laws in this country but not many to protect us against the rich.

Anyone who says,
"It's all good,"
obviously doesn't pay attention.

EITHER YOU FIND A WAY TO DEAL WITH
THE IGNORANCE OF YOUR FELLOW MAN
OR YOU GO INSANE.

Global Warning
Humanity knows it's committing suicide
but it has no control over itself.

If anyone can
"make it"
in America,
why is it that so many don't.

Roberta is my Yoko Ono.

I am proud to say that when I die,
I will die with many opinions
but zero indoctrinated beliefs.

I don't pray. I vote.

Boredom will be the biggest mental
health challenge of the future.

It's getting so a person can't even be
naive anymore.

WISDOM TAKES TIME.

Kindness- the quality of being friendly, generous and considerate.

Most people are common.

No one can take my life away because I've written it down.

Sometimes I feel like an eleven year old boy who hasn't been raised well.

Do you want a punishing society
or a teaching society?

If you strive to be the kindest person in the
room, any other success you achieve
will actually be success.

It takes a while but eventually
we all jowl.

Do religions get in the way
of human progress
or
are they the necessary glue that
holds societies together?

I found no real growth to be easy.

Most narrow minded people seem to enjoy
being narrow minded.

Parts of the Bible were obviously written

by bigots.

If you want to be respected
for your intellect,
cover your body.

My country told me to smoke cigarettes.

Man, that'll leave a mark on a
black man.

Jesus was the "wokest."

Being dismissive is
the opposite of kindness.

Tucker Carlson is the preppy Joe Rogan.

Everyone needs a
"That's just the way he is guy"
to put strangers at ease.

If you always believe what they tell you
to believe, who are you?

By the way,
a good vanilla ice cream
is not bland.

Season 2, Episode 26

Perry Mason
(1957–1966)

The Case of the Dangerous Dowager

"All the things that I ever learned…
Were the things I must not do.
I must not love beauty. Because I may
run off with a Neapolitan fisherman.
And if not beauty, then what?
The ugliness of drink.
Nightmare of gambling.
There's another world in drink,
Mr. Mason.
A desperate hope in gambling.
No Neapolitan fishermen."

In 100 Years

    I honestly didn't think that anyone living today would appreciate "The Shell Books." However, in the future, maybe in 30, 40 or even 100 years, I believe there will be "Shell Book" parties similar to the Tupperware parties of the 1960's and 70's. And my books will be the reason people get together in 2122.

    Don't forget to bring your copy of "A Boomer Bible" to the party.

Some thoughts from Roberta....

(Embellished by Ken)
Making these books was hard.
I wanted to quit.
I'm glad I didn't.
Ken and I knew nothing about writing,
editing and formatting when we started.
With the help of the
"Digital Navigators"
from the Arizona Public Library,
we were able to complete his pentalogy
of thought, "*The Shell Books,*" the 5
books that came to be known as
"A Boomer Bible."
We are high school educated former
drunks. High school educated from
fifty years ago.
Ken's hope was to make you
think and discuss.
My hope is that they motivate you
to do something that
YOU think is impossible.

I'm Sorry

This is for anyone that I might've hurt
during my lifetime.
Although some of you deserved it,
a lot of you didn't and ended up getting
the leftover anger that should've been
directed at the ones who did.

And to those who I

Made laugh, YOU'RE WELCOME
Comforted, YOU'RE WELCOME
Enlightened, YOU'RE WELCOME
Pleasured, YOU'RE VERY WELCOME
(and Thanks back at cha)

And Finally

If any of you have found some of my
"Thoughts" unnerving or some parts of
"A Boomer Bible" offensive,
more than likely you haven't driven the
same highways as I have nor have you
walked down the same dirt roads.
Remember in
"Crack the Shell Wide Open,"
I talked about "different scenery."
That's all it really is.
My suggestion is that you get out of your
hometown for at least a year, meet some
people who weren't raised like you and who
don't look like you. Then and only then will
you truly know who **you** are. I am not the
child of any invisible dictator who watches
every move I make. I should not have to
apologize or feel "less than" for these
feelings. And I definitely shouldn't have to
follow your particular religion's dogma.
What is freedom, if not that?
Again, I never asked anyone to
agree with me.
I promised I would be honest.
I think I've kept my promise.

In Memory of Spirit the Dog

Stick Addiction

I got a stick addition

It's a canine affliction

I gotta have it in my mouth

just like a cat with a mouse

I got a stick addiction

We always bring it in the car

and daddy throws it real far

it makes me run real fast

till I run out of gas

I got a stick addiction

Please Support Greenpeace

About the Author

K A "Ken" Champagne is a poet, traveler, wordsmith, comedian, survivor, middle child, romantic, and kid-at-heart.

POSITIVE comments welcome at:
3shellbooks@gmail.com

If you were offended, please pray for me, it won't do me any good but it might make you feel better.

Made in the USA
Las Vegas, NV
03 June 2023

72889202R00341